ABOUT THE AUTHOR

The foundation for this book by Robert Swope, Jr. began in Swope's early youth in the 1950s while he was growing up in rural Central Pennsylvania. While everyone was looking up at the sky during the space race, Swope was looking down, looking down at the ground for fossils, Indian artifacts, and colonial relics. He explored the fields surrounding Watsontown, Dewart, and Warrior Run searching for artifacts. Always interested in history he did his ninth grade history paper on Indians of Pennsylvania. As a youth, he played in the Watsontown Park, went to the Watson Theatre every Friday night, swam in the river in the summers, and attended dances at Watsontown High School. As a member of Watsontown Boy Scout Troop 610, he became scout leader Bob Merrill's first Eagle Scout. He graduated from Warrior Run High School, the district which includes Watsontown, McEwensville and Delaware Township. During the 1970s Swope metal detected colonial and early settlement sites of these areas. He once lived in a Watsontown third floor apartment overlooking the river where he wrote history related magazine articles and worked on his first books. Having earned degrees from Susquehanna University and Bucknell University, Swope taught English at Warrior Run for eight years before relocating to Virginia to study Civil War history. He often gave presentations to various relic and artifact clubs and civic organizations.

About fifteen years ago, Robert Swope began studying his family history and the history of his home area. He began collecting paper items, especially real photo postcards from Turbotville and Watsontown. He learned that his great uncle, James Bannen Swope, was a postcard photographer in the early 1900s. He also knew that his eighth grade school teacher, Neoska Campbell, was the daughter of postcard photographer Ralph Fuller. Swope, in his youth, knew these two photographers. By interviewing family members and interviewing Neoska before her death in 2002, plus investigating local source material, he was able to assemble a history of these two men. Eventually, Swope expanded his quest to preserve and document the early twentieth century photo postcards from his home area in Central Pennsylvania. The result is the publishing of this book, *Watsontown, McEwensville and Delaware Township: A Real Photo Postcard History.*

Robert Swope, Jr. and Buffy.

Published by
Heritage Trails
P.O. Box 184
New Hope, Va. 24469

ISBN 0-936441-04-6

Front Cover: Postcard view of Main Street,
Watsontown, Pennsylvania.

Modern era or "Now" photographs by
author Robert Swope, Jr.

Maps and sketches by Robert McClure.

Cover design by Jared Echols.

WATSONTOWN,
McEWENSVILLE,
AND
DELAWARE TOWNSHIP:
A REAL PHOTO POSTCARD
HISTORY

By Robert Swope, Jr.

Pennsylvania Real Photo Postcard Series
Book 1

Heritage Trails
New Hope, Virginia
2006

DEDICATION

Roy Shoop was an historian. That was what Reverend W. Stevens Shipman said of him as he opened his eulogy at Roy's funeral on May 5, 2003. Though Roy Shoop was well known throughout the postcard collecting community from Canada to Florida, these words characterized him best. He was first an historian. The postcards he collected for years were vignettes of history, a means to an end, the end being a better understanding and preservation of local history. Long before the real photo postcard hobby was highly popularized, Roy was attending estate auctions in his hometown of Watsontown, Pennsylvania, and surrounding area, always on the lookout for postcards to add to his collection. In later years he attended the major postcard shows in eastern Pennsylvania. In the winters, Roy traveled to Florida and attended the Florida shows each January and February. He always returned to Pennsylvania in time for the Morlatton Show held each March. He rarely missed a major show.

Roy Shoop and his daughter Vicki took dozens of slides of his Watsontown postcards and then of modern Watsontown, so that he could give "then and now" slide presentations. Each October at the Warrior Run Heritage Days, Roy was featured in the basement of the barn where he presented his albums of postcards to Heritage Days visitors. He gave talks to clubs and community organizations, and his home was always open to visitors who came to talk postcards and view his collection.

In 2002 Roy and I got the idea for this book and a series of books on local postcards of Central Pennsylvania. We were working together on the Watsontown volume when he was stricken with a heart attack. He never recovered, and it was left to me to finish this book using as a nucleus his outstanding collection. This book is dedicated to Roy Shoop.

Roy Shoop *at the beach*

TABLE OF CONTENTS

The Lewisburg, Milton, and Watsontown Railway *trolley summer car. Harold Nesbit photo.*

THE PENNSYLVANIA REAL PHOTO POSTCARD SERIES

The purpose of the Pennsylvania Real Photo Postcard Series is to document and preserve the black and white photographic postcards of Pennsylvania's rural photographers of the early twentieth century. Some of the postcards are quite rare, perhaps only two or three of a given image are known to exist. Others are plentiful, well known in a local geographic area. By publishing these images, the art and history of the photographers are preserved for future generations.

The photographers had an important role in the peaceful early 1900s in rural America. They documented a way of life that began to disappear during WWI and was totally lost by the Great Depression. With their cameras they captured small town streets, parades and picnics, lumbering and agriculture, transportation, and places of business. They preserved a simplistic way of life that ended by the 1930s

The Pennsylvania Real Photo Postcard Series hosts some of these photographers and showcases their work. The bulk of known biographical material about a photographer is presented in the book hosting his home area. A smaller amount of biographical material about him may be repeated in another book if he traveled to that area and took photographs there also. However, *no photographic material* printed in one book is repeated in another.

A number of cabinet photos were used in this book to supplement the photo postcard material. Cabinet photos were in style from about 1866 to the mid 1920s. Loosely defined, they were professional photographs applied to heavy cardboard stock to keep the photos from curling. They were phased out by the postcard photographer and the amateur snapshot photographer.

ACKNOWLEDGMENTS

A number of people contributed to the production of this book. Foremost, I extend my thanks to Roy Shoop's adult children, Vicki, Frank, and Susan for allowing me the opportunity to scan Roy's collection of Watsontown, McEwensville, and Delaware Township postcards. In addition several people helped by providing the local history and information behind some of the postcards: Jane Shuman, Byron Parker, Jr., Craig Russell, Dart Becker, Leonard Swope, Pastor John E. Lee, and Janet Hause. Others contributed additional postcards or photographs: (Note: To ensure security and privacy, contributers' names are not listed in the captions with the images.) Harry Carson, Ron Dingle, Bob Franks, Marlin Thomas, Ruth Thomas, Michelle Webb, Alan Nauman, Ned Cook, and Jean Narber Underwood. I give special thanks to Sharon Cronrath Herald for sharing the Ruth Sechler Koch photo archives and the Cronrath family photo archives and for providing details of Watsontown. Sharon also reviewed the final draft for accuracy. Information about the photographers was contributed by: Don Brown of the Institute of American Deltiology, the late Neoska Fuller Campbell, daughter of Ralph Fuller, Anne Lipe, granddaughter of Nelson Caulkins, Marvin Wolfe, formerly of Slate Run, Jerry and Ronnie Yothers of Waterville, Pa., Helen Schuyler of Lewis Township, Harold McCollin of Watsontown, Frederick Lowell Swope and Paul Swope, sons of James Bannen Swope, Lester Swope, nephew of James Bannen Swope, Peg Maraat, granddaughter of James Bannen Swope, and Josephine Nesbit, daughter-in-law of Harold Nesbit. In addition, I thank Robert McClure, who not only did the sketches and maps for this book, but behind the scenes was my computer consultant. I also thank Jared Echols for assisting with the computer layout. Finally, I thank my immediate family for accompanying me on many research trips and helping me with the computer work.

INTRODUCTION

By the time the postcard photographers arrived in the early twentieth century, Watsontown, McEwensville, and Delaware Township offered a wealth of photographic topics. Watsontown was a small, rural town situated on a scenic river. There, photographers could choose as subjects, historic landmarks, vintage churches, local businesses, trains and trolleys, historic homes, celebrations, and parades. Watsontown was such an archetypal pre WWI community that one might think that Norman Rockwell was inspired by its slice of Americana. McEwensville had its own nostalgia; churches, schools, old houses, and shaded streets. Delaware Township, which included the town of Dewart, had a hotel, a train station, churches, and two historic events, a tornado and a train wreck. A host of postcard photographers captured the spirit of these golden era communities in scores of real photo postcards.

Watsontown is a small town along the West Branch of the Susquehanna River in Northumberland County, Pennsylvania. As a small town it is exceptionally historical, for its birth and growth and the birth and growth of our nation are one and the same. Watsontown was hewn from the frontier wilderness. Revolutionary War battles were fought within a few miles of this seemingly insignificant point along the Great Shamokin Path. After the Revolutionary War, Watsontown would emerge and grow along this trail.

In the post Revolutionary War period there was a natural evolution of going from unsettled turmoil to settlement and commerce in America. Watsontown was part of this. Following the establishment of Watsontown, business emerged and grew. Taverns, blacksmith shops, and stores were built. During the early 1800s, nearby McEwensville was established. Later, the first half of the nineteenth century saw the arrival of the canal and the railroad. During this time Delaware Township was formed and Dewart grew as a community. Business in these communities followed the same path of advancing industrialization as in most American small towns. By the end of the Civil War, there was no stopping or even slowing down progress. Factories evolved, community

Main Street in Watsontown, *circa 1912 real photo postcard. In the center of the street is the trolley.*

government grew, and building and development took place everywhere. By the end of the nineteenth century Watsontown, McEwensville, and Delaware Township were rich with both heritage and modernization. The postcard photographer, whose purpose was to take photographs he could sell, could capitalize on a treasure trove of subject material.

The Pennsylvania Real Photo Postcard Series hosts Watsontown, McEwensville and Delaware Township in Book 1 of the series. Notable postcard photographers were Lester Deininger, Nelson Caulkins, James Bannen Swope, and Ralph Fuller. Deininger was prolific in capturing Dewart and Watsontown events, and Caulkins captured the spirit of Watsontown in its parades and festivities. Swope and Fuller, both resident Turbotville photographers, made many postcards of McEwensville and Delaware Township. Several other photographers are mentioned for their contribution to the photo history of the area.

Included in this book is a very brief history of the communities. The purpose of this history is to provide a concise background to the postcards. There are many sources that provide a detailed history of Watsontown, McEwensville, and Delaware Township, and certainly more to be written. The purpose of this book is not to compete with these works but to complement them, that is, to provide a photographic history of the area, from a time when postcards were the "in" thing and the postcard photographer was a well known and often seen man about town. Enjoy the nostalgia, for this era will never be gone with the wind as long as the works of these men survive.

South Main Street, *Watsontown, in the early twentieth century. Real photo postcard.*

CHAPTER 1
THE PHOTOGRAPHERS

Before 1907, postal regulations did not allow the address and the message to be written on the same side of the postcard. The message was written on the front (at that time called the back), and the address was written on the back (then called the front). Though there certainly were real photo postcards before 1907, part of the photo side of the card was left white for a message and the photo was often defaced with writing. The new regulations of 1907 allowed the message to be written on the same side as the address on what is called a divided back. The right side was reserved for the address, while the left side was used for the message. The front of the postcard could remain untouched. The new regulation allowed an excellent forum for the photographer - a full postcard size photograph. The photographer captured the image on an appropriate size glass negative, and then made a contact print (real photo) on postcard stock. He had an entity he could market and sell, the real photo postcard. He made souvenir photographs of places, portraits of families, and photos of keynote events. Whereas the "woods photographers" of the 1800s had a limited market, this new generation of photographers had a world market,

as sending and collecting postcards became a popular fad.

The postcard photographer turned to a broad subject range. He captured small town life, parades, celebrations, buildings, parks, trolleys, and even children and dogs. Wherever he could capture scenes he could sell, he would be there to take pictures. In doing so, the postcard photographer preserved an endearing era of small town America.

Of the numerous photographers that photographed Watsontown, McEwensville, and Delaware Township, four stand out. They are: the great Pine Creek photographer, Nelson Caulkins, a talented and prolific Turbotville photographer, Ralph Fuller, another young man from Turbotville, James Bannen Swope, and in the later part of the real photo postcard era, Watsontown's Lester Deininger. Together these men account for many of the identified photo postcards in this book.

The amount of biographical material about a photographer in a Pennsylvania Real Photo Series book is commensurate with the amount of his identified postcards within that geographic area. Fuller and Swope, for example, are discussed in even more detail in the Turbotville book, as they were

Undivided back, the message was written on the front or photo side. Though this type originated before 1907, its use continued well into the divided back era.

Divided back. Postal regulations of 1907 allowed the message to be written on the same side as the address. The full front could be used for a photograph.

Turbotville photographers. Caulkins is discussed more fully in the Pine Creek book, for he worked much of his life in that area, having lived in Watsontown only a few years. What little is known of Deininger is told here, for most of his postcard work was done in Watsontown and Dewart. This chapter concludes with a limited discussion of additional photographers who contributed only a few photo postcards or photographs to this area.

NELSON A. CAULKINS

Nelson Adelbert Caulkins was born November 29, 1874 in Unidella, New York. He began his professional photography business in the Baltimore - Washington area, but left abruptly to take lumbering photographs in the Pine Creek watershed north of Jersey Shore, Pennsylvania. From 1904 to 1908 Caulkins maintained a studio at Slate Run and lived at nearby Cammal (1), both lumbering communities in the Pine Creek Valley, a part of which later became known as the Pennsylvania Grand Canyon. During his early career Caulkins traveled to New York State where he lived with and photographed the Seneca Indians. He was made an honorary chief and in later years his studio was adorned

with his professionally done portrait enlargements of the Senecas (2). However, most of his life was spent in the Pine Creek watershed. All the while he lived in the Pine Creek area, Caulkins was an ardent, incessant photographer. Using his camera to make a living, Caulkins traveled up and down the Pine Creek Valley, east and west to other watersheds such as Lycoming and Loyalsock Creeks, and north to Tioga and Mansfield. He rarely traveled south, rarely except for the three years that he lived in Watsontown. During these years, 1917 - 1919, he captured with his camera some of the most outstanding images for real photo postcards ever done in Pennsylvania.

In 1900 Nelson Caulkins married Jessie Blanche Thatcher. The Caulkins had six children between 1901 and 1914. Sometime before May of 1917 the Caulkins moved to Watsontown where they lived briefly at the Mansion House before finding a house in town (3). Two of the children, Frank and Thelma, are featured in Caulkins' Watsontown photographs. Caulkins set up a studio and store, and served for a time as justice of the peace. Thelma, a pretty young girl, was considered "the belle of Watsontown (4)."

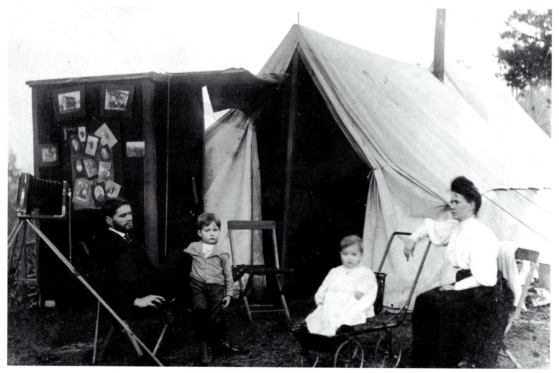

Nelson Caulkins, *a Pine Creek photographer who lived in Watsontown from 1917 to 1919. This circa 1906 photograph was taken near Slate Run. Shown are Nelson Caulkins, his two children, Albert and Frank, and wife Jessie.*

Nelson Caulkins' parlor in Watsontown. *Caulkins, in addition to his photography business, also served as justice of the peace.*

In the autumn of 1918 and winter of 1919, the Spanish flu pandemic swept the United States killing ten times more Americans than the Great War. On October 25 of 1918 Jessie Caulkins died of the influenza. After his wife died Caulkins continued his work in photography. (5)

While in Watsontown, Caulkins remarried, this time to a Watsontown lady named Bertha. The marriage was brief for she died a year later. Caulkins left Watsontown and moved to Williamsport where he briefly established a souvenir business. Eventually he returned to the Pine Creek watershed.

While in Watsontown, from 1917 to 1919, Caulkins photographed July 4th parades, Flag Raising Day, the Dewart cyclone or tornado damage, and the Dewart train wreck. During the time Caulkins was in Watsontown, he also photographed Turbotville, McEwensville, Dewart, and Lewisburg. Only the Watsontown, Dewart, and McEwensville real photo postcards are featured in this book.

After Nelson Caulkins left Williamsport and returned to the Pine Creek Valley, he set up a studio and photo lab in Morris, a small town on Babb Creek in southern Tioga County. From there

Caulkins traveled the Pennsylvania Grand Canyon continuously, looking for the perfect photograph. He once climbed a mountain near Slate Run, but the light was not just right for a photograph, and so he descended the mountain without snapping a photograph (6).

Caulkins' photo postcards have been published by Ellinger of Williamsport, Pa., G.V. Millar & Co., of Scranton, Pa., the Wellsboro Chamber of Commerce, and the Pennsylvania Tourist Commission. Mostly, though, even beyond the end of the real photo postcard era in the 1920s, Caulkins printed his own real photo postcards and sold them as souvenirs. His beautiful contact prints of the early years show up as white border postcards from the 1920s through the 1950s.

In 1927 Nelson Caulkins married Margaret "Maggie" Ammerman, a widow with nine children. The couple remained married until Margaret's death in 1956. (7)

In the 1950s Caulkins maintained a studio in Waterville where Pine Creek and Little Pine Creek meet. He worked from a house, formerly Brown's Store, that doubled as a photo studio and souvenir shop, located on Little Pine Creek at the northwestern foot of the Route 44 bridge. There, with John Somerville, he made wooden souvenirs of

Nelson Caulkins, his third wife Maggie, and his dog Togo. *This photograph appears to have been taken in the late 1930s.*

Three of Nelson Caulkins' daughters, *Nellie, Thelma and Fay. Photograph circa 1928.*

the Pennsylvania Grand Canyon and sold his post-cards. During some of this time Caulkins continued his residence in Morris where he also maintained a lab and studio.

On October 6, 1958 a devastating fire destroyed Caulkins' store and studio in Waterville. At that point he was 83 years old, and the fire that destroyed his negatives, cameras, and only prints of the Senecas, also ended his photography. Though he still had zeal for family life, he was no longer able to maintain the drive and enthusiasm for photography that were once the hallmarks of his career. He died in 1965 at the age of 90. (8)

RALPH FULLER

Ralph Waldo Emerson Fuller was born July 5, 1884. He grew up on a farm in the Muncy Hills four miles north of Turbotville and about nine miles northeast of Watsontown. He and his brother kept bees for honey. His father, Otis C. Fuller was a school board member in Lewis Township. When Ralph Fuller was 23 he moved into Turbotville and opened a photography business in 1907. At the north end of town near the railroad station Ralph bought a small store and also operated a horse-drawn photography wagon. (9)

From his base of operations in Turbotville, Ralph Fuller traveled the local countryside looking for suitable topics for postcard photography. His main geographic area stretched from Washingtonville to Turbotville and McEwensville, but he also took photographs in Watsontown, Allenwood, Muncy, Danville, and Lairdsville. His subjects ranged from family gatherings to views of towns, buildings, and events. Some of his views appear to be made in great numbers, whereas others are rare, perhaps even unique. During his life he rarely traveled. He made a few trips to New York City, Atlantic City and Niagara Falls and made real photo postcards of each place. Otherwise, he mainly worked within Northumberland and Montour Counties. Fuller was a local photographer in the esthetic sense, for his views are comprised of all the ingredients of small town life, shaded streets, rural saw mills, parades, town plays and locally important buildings.

In April of 1913 Ralph Fuller married Dema Shade, whose parents owned and operated a general store next to Ralph's photo studio. In March of 1914 Ralph and Dema Fuller had their only child, Catherine Neoska Fuller.

By the 1920s the real photo postcard era was nearing an end. Fuller adjusted by taking on an International Harvester dealership and a Purina franchise. His once active photo studio became a full-fledged hardware store. (10)

Ralph Fuller was an innovator and entrepreneur. He was one of the first in Turbotville to own an automobile. He was the first to own a radio. He operated a silver fox farm behind his hardware store. (11)

In the late years of his life he fell to ill health, became a near invalid, and remained closed in his home until his death in 1977. He wrote before his death that he only had a rural education, having attended "the red country schoolhouse," and that he spent his entire life in Northumberland County (12). Though his admissions of his life were modest, his deeds were great. Ralph Fuller captured with his camera a golden era that was here for a moment and then gone.

Ralph Fuller, *as a young man in the early 1900s. Real photo postcard.*

Ralph Fuller's daughter Neoska and her dog. Fuller snapshot, circa 1928.

Neoska Fuller, daughter of Ralph Fuller, circa 1932. This is a Deininger portrait. By this time, Fuller was no longer in the portrait business, however he continued to take informal snapshots.

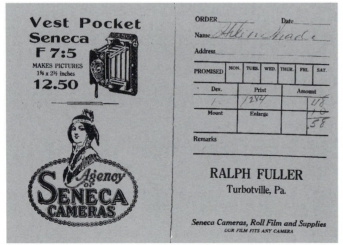

Ralph Fuller film envelope from his studio in Turbotville.

Portrait of Ralph Fuller. Cabinet photo.

6

Ralph Fuller, *on the left, in front of his store at 37 Main Street, Turbotville, in the early 1900s. In the background to the left is the Turbotville railroad station. Photograph.*

Ralph Fuller *in his car, one of the first cars in Turbotville, 1908 Fuller photograph.*

Ralph Fuller's store *in Turbotville. The photo studio has become a hardware store. Snapshot taken New Year's Day, 1935.*

The lot next to Ralph Fuller's store *in Turbotville displays farm equipment. Fuller became an International Harvester dealer in 1918. This snapshot was taken from the rear corner of Fuller's store, looking across Main Street toward the northwest. In the background is Dye's Mill.*

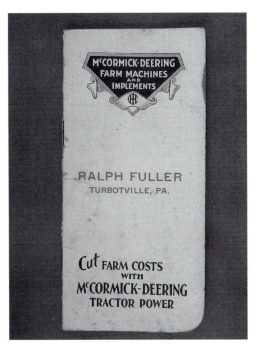

A leather luggage tag with *Ralph Fuller's signature.*

A 1932 McCormick-Deering calendar booklet from Ralph Fuller's store in Turbotville. At the bottom of the McCormick-Deering logo is the International Harvester symbol. McCormick Harvesting Machine Company and Deering Harvester Company merged in 1902 to form International Harvester. Fuller sold International equipment until 1938.

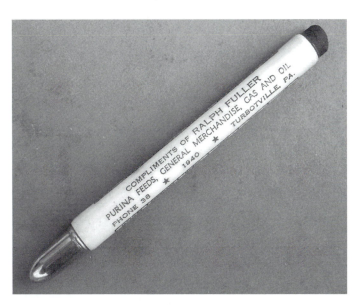

A 1940 Ralph Fuller advertising pencil from his store in Turbotville. Fuller became a Ralston Purina dealer in 1926.

9

JAMES BANNEN SWOPE

Two brothers from Turbotville, James Bannen Swope and Roy Wagner Swope, made a brief but significant contribution to the postcard photography of the West Branch Valley. James Bannen Swope, born 1883, generally dropped his first name and went by his middle name Bannen. Of the two brothers, James Bannen Swope is regarded as the photographer whereas Roy Swope assisted and promoted sales. (13) Though family history attributes the camera work to James Bannen Swope, he apparently considered himself and Roy to be a team. Many of the signed postcards are labeled "Swope Bro's." These men were the great uncles of the author of this book. (Author's note: Retired Air Force Sergeant Roy William Swope (1925 - 2004) who lived in the stone tavern in Delaware Township near Turbotville was the nephew of Roy Wagner Swope (1887 - 1940) discussed in this chapter.)

The Swope brothers were sons of Fred Swope, a school director from Lewis Township. Fred Swope served on the school board with Ralph Fuller's father Otis Fuller. In 1904 Otis Fuller was president of the board while Fred Swope was treasurer. Ralph Fuller and James Bannen Swope knew each other, but to what extent they worked together or competed with each other is unknown. At one point, Hugh Swope, a brother of James Bannen and Roy Swope, worked for Ralph Fuller. (14)

James Bannen Swope graduated in 1903 from Turbotville High School. Two years later he confronted his father about attending Susquehanna University, a Lutheran affiliated college in Selinsgrove, Pa. Fred Swope was opposed to the idea, saying that James Bannen was making too much money in photography to quit. James Bannen Swope insisted that he heard the call to ministry, and that he planned to continue to seminary school after he finished his education at Susquehanna. His father then encouraged him to use his photography, especially in the summers, to help pay for his schooling. Bannen Swope continued his photography, putting himself through Susquehanna University and Gettysburg Seminary School. He graduated from seminary school in 1912 and that

James Bannen Swope, *a Turbotville photographer who made real photo postcards of McEwensville and Delaware Township. Swope real photo postcard.*

James Bannen Swope and Margaret Yeager Swope, *shortly after their marriage in 1912. Swope real photo postcard.*

year married his Susquehanna sweetheart Margaret Yeager of Halifax, Pa. That year Bannen Swope answered the call to minister at Trinity Lutheran Church in Kalamazoo, Michigan. After three years in Michigan, he accepted an invitation to be the pastor at the Trinity Evangelical Lutheran Church in Chicago Heights, Illinois. The couple raised four boys in Illinois. Reverend James Bannen Swope remained in the Lutheran Church in Chicago Heights until his death in 1976. (15)

James Bannen Swope worked as a photographer in the Susquehanna Valley from about 1906 until 1912. But, in the short time he was involved, he took photographs of Turbotville, Dewart, McEwensville, and Watsontown. His photo postcards include churches, community buildings, baseball teams, and town streets. Many of Swope's real photo postcards are not signed but can be determined to be his by his unique writing style. Had James Bannen Swope not gone into the ministry, he may have done even more great photography. But then, he would have left undone the work he did as a minister. He married hundreds of couples and advised thousands of parishioners. His son Paul Swope wrote, "James Bannen Swope felt called into the ministry and as such was a true pastor to his flock, always providing education, solace, and comfort, and assisting any of his parishioners in any way he could (16)."

James Bannen Swope lived the life of a pastor and will be remembered in Chicago Heights and by his family for his devotion to the ministry. But, in Pennsylvania, he had another history also, that of a dedicated, talented photographer who left behind a legacy of excellent photographic postcard material.

Four Generations: *James Bannen Swope standing, his mother Mary Bannen Swope, his grandfather James Bannen, and his son Frederick Lowell Swope. Real photo postcard, 1917.*

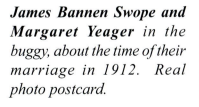

James Bannen Swope and Margaret Yeager *in the buggy, about the time of their marriage in 1912. Real photo postcard.*

The Trinity Evangelical Lutheran Church in Chicago Heights, Illinois. James Bannen Swope spent most of his life in the ministry in this church after he left Turbotville. Bannen Swope snapshot, circa 1926.

Margaret Yeager's Junior Class photograph from Susquehanna University. She was in the graduating class of 1910.

Car owned by James Bannen Swope after he left Turbotville. Swope snapshot.

Roy Wagner Swope, brother of James Bannen Swope, helped print the postcards and handled the sales. He taught at the one-room school at Five Points in Lewis Township before leaving for a career in city engineering in the Midwest. He died in Kansas City, Missouri in 1940 under mysterious circumstances.

Signature of James Bannen Swope.

LESTER DEININGER

Lester Deininger, born in 1881, was Watsontown's resident photographer. From the late teens through the 1940s Deininger did portrait work, commercial photography, and photo processing in his studio and lab in the Farmers National Bank building in the 100 block of Main Street, Watsontown. Though his main work was portrait and group photography, Deininger made some excellent postcard views of the area. An example of his best work was a series of five postcards of the cyclone damage at Dewart in 1919.

Lester Deininger and his wife Hazel lived in a modest stucco house on East First Street across from the Watson Inn. Deininger was a member of the First Presbyterian Church and the West Branch Volunteer Fire Company. He died in 1954 and was buried in the Watsontown Cemetery. (17)

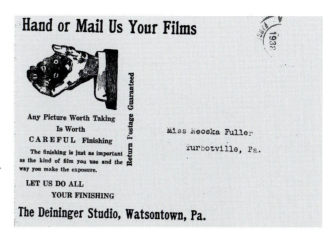

Envelope from the Deininger Studio in Watsontown. *This is addressed to Neoska Fuller, daughter of photographer Ralph Fuller. By the late 1920s Ralph Fuller outsourced some of his black and white work to Deininger.*

Now: House on First Street across from the Watson Inn where Lester Deininger lived while he was a photographer in Watsontown. Photographed by the author, 2006.

13

The Sovereign Bank building *at 109 Main Street, Watsontown, as photographed by the author in 2006. Formerly called the Farmers' National Bank, this building once held the portrait studio of Lester Deininger.*

Devitt's Camp in White Deer Valley *near Watsontown and Dewart. This is a Deininger real photo postcard postmarked 1915. Dr. William Devitt of Philadelphia established the camp in 1912 as a treatment center for tuberculosis patients.*

JOHN WILSON

Born in October of 1863, John Wilson was a seasoned photographer approaching middle age at the time Fuller, Swope, and Deininger were just beginning their careers. He was responsible for several of the postcard views of Riverside Park south of Watsontown as well as hundreds of Milton area portraits and postcards. Wilson attended public schools in Montoursville in Lycoming County. He graduated from Williamsport Commercial College in 1886. Later, he married Fannie Heddons of Washingtonville in Montour County where he had a studio for a short time. (18)

Wilson moved to Milton in 1899 and initially set up his studio at 644 Lincoln Street. In 1903 he moved his studio to the J.R. Smith building on North Front Street where he remained during the rest of his career. His residence was at 57 Bound Avenue. (19)

Sketch *of John F. Wilson, Milton photographer.*

Wilson real photo postcard *of William Wagner Cronrath of Watsontown.*

Wilson portrait *of two women.*

15

Wilson real photo postcard *view of the Susquehanna River looking north toward Watsontown.*

Wilson real photo postcard of the Milton Fair, *dated 1906. The fair was held north of Milton on the road to Watsontown.*

THE FOSNOTS

Lew Cass Fosnot was born in Cumberland County in 1848. At the age of 15 he enlisted in the Union Army and served in the Civil War. He was discharged from the Army of the James in 1866. In the mid 1870s he moved to Watsontown to work in the newspaper business. In 1890 Lew Fosnot became sole owner of the Watsontown newspaper, the Record and Star. For decades Fosnot, as chief editor of his paper, pressed the local and state politicians to finance and build a bridge from White Deer on the west bank of the Susquehanna River to Watsontown on the east bank. This task did not see fruition until 1928, eight years after Fosnot's death. (20)

In 1898, Lew Fosnot made his son, John Clyde Fosnot, a partner in ownership of the Record and Star. After his father's death in 1920, John Clyde Fosnot became the champion voice for the proponents of a White Deer - Watsontown bridge. (21)

The Fosnot name appears as photographer on two of the Riverside Park postcard views taken south of Watsontown. As to which Fosnot it was that took the photographs is a matter of conjecture.

Close-up of the front *of Fosnot's Record and Star Printing House on Main Street in the Watsontown Boot and Shoe building.*

Sketch of Lew and John Fosnot *and the White Deer – Watsontown bridge.*

17

LEWIS D. THOMAS

Lewis D. Thomas was born in 1883 and grew up near Spring Garden, a small hamlet in Union County across the Susquehanna River from Dewart and west of the river town of Allenwood. In 1903 at the age of 20 he received a Century Grand camera from his mother as a gift and soon after began a professional photography career. (22)

Lewis Thomas had a sister Susan, who was married and living in New York State in the early twentieth century. So that she would not feel far from home, "Lewis took pictures of the valley, which he printed as picture post cards, and mailed them up there (to his sister in New York)." Susan died suddenly in January of 1909, soon after having given birth to a daughter. From these events, it is known that Thomas was making real photo postcards prior to January of 1909. (23)

In 1911 Lewis Thomas married Mary Ellen Reaser. From 1912 to 1917 Thomas worked for the Swanger Studio (pronounced Swunger) on Broadway in Milton, Pa. Some of the Swanger signed postcards were taken by Thomas. In March of 1917, after being pressed by his relatives to take over the family farm, he left the Swanger Studio and returned to Spring Garden. For the next two decades Thomas was in and out of farming with various degrees of success. During the 1920s and 1930s he and his wife raised eight children while fighting the hardships brought on by the Great Depression. Photography was not part of his life during this time. (24)

By World War II Thomas and his family had settled down in a house he had bought in Dewart in 1927. During the 1940s he reopened his professional business in Dewart, but by that time the adventurous era of the postcard photographer was over. His business consisted of mostly local portrait work.

Lewis Thomas was a gifted photographer whose career was cut short by family stress and hardship. His signed postcard work consists of Spring Valley, Allenwood, and the surrounding White Deer Valley. He is mentioned here because of his association with Dewart and the fact that he may have taken some unsigned views of Delaware Township. He is not associated with the Thomas photographers of Shamokin in Northumberland County. (25)

Lewis Thomas real photo postcard *of a steam engine and thrashing machine in the White Deer Valley, circa 1910. (See Thomas, Lewey and Mary Ellen, Moving On, for additional postcards by Lewis Thomas.)*

Lewis D. Thomas, *a White Deer Valley postcard photographer who eventually settled in Dewart. In 1911 Thomas married Mary Ellen Reaser who lived near Spring Garden.*

Thomas Photo Shop *envelope from Dewart. Thomas did portrait work in Dewart in the 1940s.*

THOMAS PHOTO SHOP
Everything In Pictures

Phone   No. 722
Name
Address

Roll	Pack	Size	Size	Finish
				DULL
Duplicates	Each	Prints		GLOSS

Developing			Dr.	Cr.
Film				
Prints				
Prints				
Enlargement				
Copy				
Tint				
Total				

DEVELOPING	ENLARGING	PORTRAITS
PRINTING	COPYING	TINTING

Mail orders given prompt attention

L. D. Thomas & Son
Box 101   Dewart, Pennsylvania

A farm scene in White Deer Valley. *Real photo postcard, circa 1910, by Lewis Thomas.*

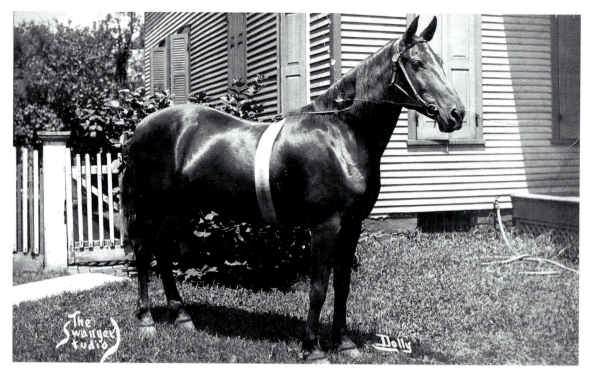

A horse named Dolly, circa 1914. *This real photo postcard showing the Swanger Studio photographer's mark was taken by Lewis Thomas. Thomas also made postcards of Devitt's Camp which were signed Swanger. In addition to his Thomas-signed postcards of Spring Garden, he made unsigned postcards of various scenes in the White Deer Valley, Allenwood, and Elimsport.*

The covered bridge at Spring Garden. *Thomas real photo postcard, circa 1910.*

HAROLD NESBIT

In the summer of 2005 several photo albums were sold at an estate sale in Milton, Pa. Most of the albums consisted of local photographs printed on postcard size photographic paper, though none appeared to be printed as postcards. All of the photographs were identified as to subject, location and approximate date. These photos were taken by Harold Nesbit, an area farmer who lived in a large brick house overlooking the Susquehanna River south of Milton. They dated to the late 1800s and early 1900s and included the Lewisburg, Milton and Watsontown Passenger Railway trolley, the July 4, 1922 parade in Milton, the Pennsylvania Canal, various farming topics, and of particular interest, the 1928 White Deer - Watsontown Bridge opening ceremony and parade. (26)

Nesbit married at the age of 65. He was a member of the First Presbyterian Church on Walnut Street in Milton. In his later years before his death, he lived on Broadway in Milton. His old, stately farmhouse still stands next to Robbins Marine two miles south of Milton on Route 405. (27)

It appears Nesbit was always an accomplished amateur photographer, never a professional. However, as an amateur the quality of his photography was exceptional. His selection of subject material, his angle of exposure, and his quality of composition separated his work from that of the casual snapshooter. Today much of his scenic work displays an eerie loneliness combined with nostalgic sentiment. He is mentioned here for his photographic documentation of the bridge ceremony and of the Watsontown trolley.

Harold Nesbit as a young man. Portrait taken in 1896.

Harold Nesbit in later years. Photograph taken May 14, 1930.

21

Early photo *of the Lewisburg, Milton, and Watsontown Railway trolley taken by Harold Nesbit between 1890 and 1907.*

Bridge over the Pennsylvania Canal. *Photo taken by Harold Nesbit, March 19, 1903.*

The opening of the White Deer – Watsontown bridge, July 4, 1928. Photo taken by Harold Nesbit. (See Franks & Houser, A Landmark Reborn, for additional photos by Nesbit of the bridge opening.)

The day of the bridge opening, July 4, 1928. Nesbit photo.

A parade across the White Deer – Watsontown bridge *on opening day, July 4, 1928. Nesbit photo.*

Parade on South Main Street, *Watsontown, celebrating the opening of the bridge, July 4, 1928. Nesbit photo.*

View of the White Deer – Watsontown bridge *taken from Watsontown Park. Harold Nesbit photo, July 4, 1928.*

The West Branch Transit Company bus *on its maiden run. Photographed on the river road (now Route 405) by Harold Nesbit, July 31, 1928.*

Workmen *on the trolley line. Nesbit photo.*

The last trolley *to run on the LM&W Railway, July 31, 1928. Nesbit photo.*

The Nesbit house in snow, *February 4, 1900. Nesbit photo.*

Harold Nesbit's house, July 4, 1902. *This house still stands next to Robbins Marine south of Milton. Nesbit photo.*

CHAPTER 2
WATSONTOWN

Watsontown began as an intersection in the frontier wilderness along the West Branch of the scenic Susquehanna River in Pennsylvania's Northumberland County. In 1769 the land upon which Watsontown was established was granted to two lieutenants, Daniel Hunsicker and Nicholas Housegger, as a reward for their participation in the French and Indian War. (1) The Great Shamokin Path extended from Sunbury, along the east bank of the West Branch of the Susquehanna, through the lieutenants' land, and then proceeded to Muncy.

Though the region was wilderness, it was not entirely desolate. Roads, which often followed the route of the old Indian paths, were open though not well traveled. By the beginning of the Revolutionary War, settlers had come to the West Branch Valley lured by inexpensive land and opportunity. By 1779 there were several gristmills established near the site that was soon to become Watsontown. One was located at the mouth of White Deer Creek across the Susquehanna River from Watsontown. Another was located at Jacob Freeland's land a few miles up the Warrior Run. Hawkins Boone, a cousin to Daniel Boone, established a mill at the mouth of Muddy Run two miles below Watsontown. A few miles to the east and south, was Bosley's Mill on the Chillisquaque Creek at what was later called Washingtonville. As early as 1775, church services were held at what is now

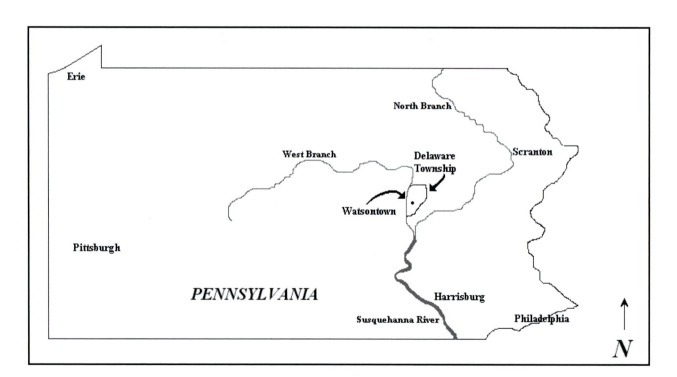

Map of Pennsylvania *showing the location of Watsontown and Delaware Township along the West Branch of the Susquehanna River.*

the Watsontown Park. Even before Watsontown was a town, the frontier surrounding the future site was being populated with settlers trying to build homes and businesses in the wilderness.

During the Revolutionary War, in July of 1779, a combined force of over 165 British soldiers and Iroquois Indians attacked Fort Freeland at Warrior Run. The fort was destroyed, the garrison killed or taken prisoner, and the women and children sent fleeing down river to Fort Augusta at Sunbury. Many settlers vacated their homes in what history has called the Second Runaway. Eventually the Continental Army eradicated the area of the British and any marauding Indians and by the end of the war in 1783 the area was becoming increasingly more settled.

With peace restored to the West Branch Valley, the settlement of a community along the river seemed to have a solid future. In 1790 a log school was built on the south end of Lieutenant Housegger's land and served as the community's only school until 1800. In 1792 John Watson bought the land that had belonged to Hunsicker and Housegger. The boundary between the two lieutenants' land formed a line perpendicular to the main road and ran from the river across that thoroughfare. In 1796 John Watson laid out a street on this line that became known as Market Street. Around the intersection of Market Street and the present Main Street the community of Watsontown began to grow. The name of the street running from the river was changed to Front Street and later to First Street. Some of the buildings from this early era are still standing. (2)

In 1801 Daniel Caldwell established a ferry between his home at White Deer and Watsontown. Eventually a ferry house for collecting tolls was built at Watsontown. The ferry house site was located in the field just above the east end of the present White Deer - Watsontown river bridge. There was no bridge at Watsontown throughout the nineteenth century, and so the ferry persisted in use for over 125 years, finally being replaced in 1928 by the present bridge. During much of its later history the ferry was owned and operated by the Bly family.

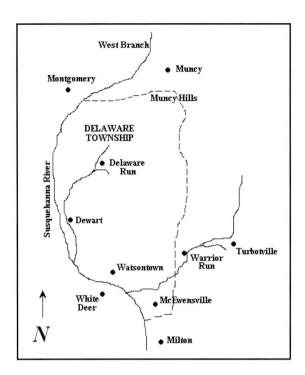

Watsontown and McEwensville surrounded by *Delaware Township. These boundaries have not changed snce the mid nineteenth century. The west boundary of Delaware Township is the Susquehanna River.*

Now: First Street, Watsontown, looking west toward the river. First Street was the original Market Street in the early nineteenth century. This photograph was taken in 2003 by the author.

29

In 1828 the West Branch Division of the Pennsylvania Canal was opened. At Watsontown the canal ran near the Susquehanna River bank between the town and the river. A towpath used for mules to tow the canal boats can still be seen at Watsontown. The Port May locks were built south of Watsontown to allow for elevation as the boats traveled up river. Commercial business on the canal began in 1830 and flourished until the Philadelphia and Erie Railroad (later the Pennsylvania Railroad) came through town in 1854. The canal continued in use into the twentieth century, but business was greatly diminished by the use of the railroad.

A number of lumber businesses were prominent in Watsontown in the 1800s. In 1856 a large lumber mill was built along the canal beginning at Fourth Street and running southward. The mill changed hands but eventually grew to include a large sawmill south of town, a planing mill, and a matchstick factory. Much of the timber came from the White Deer Creek watershed and was used for railroad construction. The large mill south of town was photographed in the early 1900s.

A planing mill called Wagner, Starr and Company was built in 1867. This evolved to be the Watsontown Planing Mill and then in the early 1900s to Watsontown Door and Sash Company. In 1937 the business was sold to Philco Corporation and became Watsontown's famous Philco Cabinet Plant.

The Watsontown Car Works was established in 1872 along Ash Street between Fourth and Seventh Streets. Though a fire terminated the busi-

Cabinet Photograph: The Pennsylvania Canal just south of Watsontown, circa 1901.

ness in 1892 the facility was activated again in 1903 as the Watsontown Foundry. The Foundry has been in continuous operation for over a century. (3)

The Watsontown Steam Tannery was located along the railroad on the north end of town. The tannery was in operation from 1866 to after the turn of the century. In the early 1900s the tannery spawned a related business called the Watsontown Boot and Shoe Company, located on Main Street between Second and Third Streets. (4)

Though in the late 1800s lumbering seemed to be the omnipresent industry in northern Pennsylvania, the area immediately around Watsontown was still predominantly agricultural. To serve the needs of area farmers, the Watsontown Steam Flour Mill was built in 1868 just east of the railroad at Eighth Street. In 1913 the business was sold and

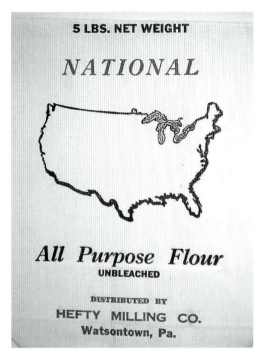

Hefty Milling Company flour bag.

Cabinet Photograph: Outdoor activities at the Watsontown Steam Tannery, circa 1901.

Cabinet Photograph: Winter scene *of the Pennsylvania Canal near the Watsontown Brick Company south of Watsontown, circa 1901.*

Cabinet Photograph: The railroad south of Watsontown *is in the left of this photograph. To the right are the locks of the Pennsylvania Canal, circa 1901.*

Cabinet Photograph: The Watsontown Nail Works *was located south of the Watsontown Park along the Susquehanna River.*

became the Hefty Milling Company. (5)

The Watsontown Nail Works began business in 1886 just south of the present Watsontown Park. Though it was no longer in operation due to a destructive fire, it was photographed just after turn of the century. (6)

Around the beginning of the nineteenth century bricks were transported from Philadelphia for the John Watson, Jr. house along the river near First Street. The builders had no idea at the time that the red shale hills around Watsontown held some of the best material in the world for making bricks. It would be the twentieth century before brick production would begin in Watsontown. The Watsontown Brick Company originated in 1907 and the Keystone Brick Company, later called Glen-Gery, was founded in 1910. These two companies made some of the highest quality bricks in America over a time span of nearly a century.

Business was only one facet of growth and de-velopment in the nineteenth century. Community organizations, churches, government and educa-tion grew in a commensurate manner. In 1859 a private academy was built on First Street. This building was later taken over by the borough and maintained as the "poor house." In 1882 the "Eighth Street School" was built at Eighth and Elm Streets. This was used for all grades until the Watsontown High School was built at Brimmer Avenue in 1924. The school at Eighth Street was used for elementary education until it was de-stroyed by fire in 1956. (7)

The churches that were photographed for post-cards in the early 1900s were built in the years following the Civil War. These structures still stand today. Though Presbyterians worshipped at the Warrior Run Church throughout the nineteenth century, Watsontown did not get a Presbyterian Church until 1874-75 when the First Presbyterian Church was built. The Trinity United Church of

*Cabinet Photograph: **The Klapp Drug Store**, circa 1911, located in Watsontown on the southeast corner of Second Street (Brimmer Avenue) and Main Street.*

Christ began as a Union Church and then later organized as a Reformed Church. The present Trinity United Church of Christ was completed in 1867. In 1872 construction of the Methodist Church on Third Street was completed. In 1886 the cornerstone was laid for the present First Lutheran Church on Main and Fourth Streets. The Baptist congregation used a white frame building from 1870 until 1897 when the First Baptist Church was completed as a brick structure. (8)

Other keynotes in progress in Watsontown in the second half of the nineteenth century included the formation of a fire company in 1873, the opening of a borough building for local government functions, and the building of two inns that are still in business today (the Mansion House and the Watson Inn). In 1867, on the southeast corner of Main and Second Streets, Minerva Hall, a theater and dance hall opened. The auditorium was on the second floor and hosted numerous period plays. The first Memorial Day celebration was held in Watsontown in 1882, sponsored by the Bryson GAR Post. (9)

Like the rest of the nation, Watsontown entered a golden era at the turn of the century. The Spanish American war was over and pleasant times were on the horizon. From 1900 to 1917 there were peace and good financial times. In 1915 the Watsontown Borough Council voted to hold an Old Home Week in August. Festivities included parades complete with mummers and floats. Various parades and celebrations were held in successive years in Watsontown. Fortunately, some were documented by one of America's great postcard photographers, Nelson Caulkins. The Caulkins' photographic postcards of Flag Raising Day and July 4th capture the zenith of small town spirit and are some of the most desired postcards of the Watsontown area.

During these carefree years the Lewisburg, Milton and Watsontown Passenger Railway Company operated a trolley from Watsontown southward along the east bank of the river to the Lewisburg bridge. Eventually, it was extended

Cabinet Photograph: Play held in the " opera house" in Watsontown. The Opera House was located on the second floor of a frame building at 225 Main Street, later the site of Werner's meat store.

Cabinet Photograph: Another view of the play at the Opera House in Watsontown, circa 1901.

Cabinet Photograph: President William McKinley's Funeral Train at Watsontown. *This historically significant photograph was taken September 16, 1901 just two days after McKinley's death. McKinley was shot by an assassin in Buffalo, New York.*

Cabinet Photograph: The 1901 Watsontown baseball team. The man second from the right in the back row is wearing a Bucknell University uniform.

Cabinet Photograph: ***A parade in Watsontown*** *at the intersection of Fifth and Elm Streets, circa late 1800s. These old veterans appear to be the right age for GAR members. The Grand Army of the Republic was the veterans' organization for Civil War veterans. Watsontown had the Bryson Post, GAR.*

Cabinet Photograph: ***The same parade*** *at Watsontown's Fifth and Elm Streets. Shown is Watsontown's horse drawn fire equipment.*

Flag Raising Day, Watsontown, Pa.,
May 12th, 17.
Photo By CAULKINS

Cabinet Photograph: *Taken* by postcard photographer, Nelson Caulkins. Shown is the Flag Raising Day Ceremony, May 12, 1917, in front of the Watsontown Door & Sash Company on Seventh Street.

through Lewisburg to Mifflinburg. The trolley track ran down the middle of Main Street, Watsontown, and made a nostalgic and endearing scene. The line passed through a popular recreational park called Riverside Park just south of Watsontown. This park had amusements, swimming, boating and romantic scenery. The trolley and the park were especially favorite topics of photographers.

By the eve of the Great Depression, the work of the postcard photographer was on the decline. Inexpensive snapshot cameras, the public's fascination with color postcards, and a focus on world rather than local events, all contributed to the phasing out of real postcard photography. Yet, while they were in town, the postcard photographers documented the past so that today's viewers can get an insight into a nostalgic era.

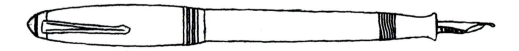

The Old Store *is the log structure in the photo just to the left of the large house in the foreground. It was John Watson's first house which was later used as a store after he built his second house, the large structure on the corner. Both were located along the canal near the river at the west end of present First Street. Real photo postcard, circa 1910.*

First Street, Watsontown. *This photograph was taken facing east with the photographer's back to Main Street, circa 1907. In the distance is the small bridge over the Pennsylvania Railroad. First Street runs perpendicular to the Susquehanna River and to Main Street. Real photo postcard.*

An artist postcard, *dated August 21, 1908, depicts the Oley School which dates to 1869 in Watsontown.*

Main Street, Watsontown, *looking south from the intersection of Third Street, circa 1910. The store on the left later became Carson's Grocery. In the next building on the left is the Record and Star Printing House. Real photo postcard.*

Main Street, Watsontown, *looking north from the intersection of Second Street (Brimmer Avenue). The building on the left corner is the Mansion House. Caulkins real photo postcard dated 1917.*

Main Street, *facing north, taken north of the intersection of Third and Main Streets. In the upper left corner is the steeple of the First Presbyterian Church. On the right side of the postcard is Diehl's Bakery, circa 1912. Just past Deihl's Bakery, the large brick building is the Miller building. In 1912 Watsontown Borough bought the Miller building for use as a town hall or borough building.*

41

The Record & Star Printing House, *an early postcard view of the newspaper office. Watsontown's newspaper, Record and Star was published under that name from 1884 to 1926 and was located in the Watsontown Boot and Shoe building on the east side of Main Street between Second and Third Streets . Later the building was occupied by Noll's Restaurant. Today the building is gone and a CVS Pharmacy and parking lot are in its place.*

Street view *of Watsontown labeled West Fourth Street, circa 1907. Here, the photographer had his back to the railroad and was facing Main Street. The steeple of the First Lutheran Church can be seen at right center of the postcard.*

Main Street, *facing north from the intersection of Sixth Street. The church on the right is the Trinity Reformed Church, now the Trinity United Church of Christ. Caulkins real photo postcard, circa 1918.*

The public water fountain *at 305 Main Street, Watsontown. The fountain was presented to the town by the Women's Christian Temperance Union in memory of Elizabeth Follmer, a former president of the group. Later, after being moved to Watsontown Memorial Park, the fountain was destroyed by vandals. Real photo postcard.*

Main Street, *Watsontown, facing south and showing a head-on view of the trolley. The fountain at 305 Main Street can be seen along the right side of the street. Real photo postcard.*

Rare snow scene *of Watsontown, real photo postcard. This postcard message was written on July 29, 1907.*

The corner of First and Main Streets *in Watsontown, postmarked 1909. This house is now gone.*

House at the corner *of Fourth and Elm Streets, circa 1915 real photo postcard. On the back is written, "Nanna Burrows."*

MAIN +BRIMMER AVE., WATSONTOWN, PA.

Then: The corner of Main Street *and Brimmer Avenue. This is a circa 1940 real photo postcard. In 1928 Second Street was renamed Brimmer Avenue in honor of W.C. Brimmer who had fought for 15 years to get the state to build the White Deer -   Watsontown bridge across the Susquehanna River.*

Now: The corner of Main Street *and Brimmer Avenue as photographed by the author in 2003.*

Then: The Watson Inn at the corner of First Street and Main Street. A circa 1940 postcard view taken from the north front corner.

Now: The Watson Inn, taken from the north front corner in 2006. Photo by the author.

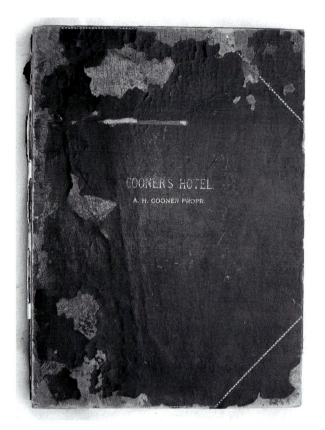

At the turn of the twentieth century the Watson Inn was called Cooner's Hotel or Cooner House, named for the first owner, William Cooner. This is the guest book from Cooner's Hotel from the late 1890s.

Page from the guest book of Cooner's Hotel, dated 1897.

Close-up of the Cooner House from a Berger published postcard from the early 1900s.

Berger's Stationery and News Depot at 144 Main Street, circa 1912 real photo postcard. *Near the top of the store window are racks of postcards for sale. Marco Berger published a number of printed photographic Watsontown postcards during this period.*

Adams' furniture store in Watsontown, circa 1910, at 128 Main Street. *The Masons met in the Masonic Hall upstairs at 126 Main Street from 1904 until 1930 when they moved to 209 – 213 Main Street. Today the store is a martial arts studio.*

Diehl's Bakery in Watsontown, circa 1912, was located on the east side of Main Street between Third and Fourth Streets where the post office is now. In addition to the store, Diehl also operated a horse-drawn bakery wagon. By 1932 the bakery had relocated to the corner of Seventh and Elm Streets. Real photo postcard.

Diehl's Bakery wagon at the store in White Deer, a village directly across the Susquehanna River from Watsontown. Real photo postcard, circa 1912.

West Side of Main Street, *a real photo postcard view taken in the 1940s. The tall brick building to the left center of the postcard was the Becker 5 & 10. Becker's store was on the west side of Main Street from about 1939 to just after WWII. The building burned in 1969, and was replaced by the Pammy J restaurant, now no longer in business.*

Now: Photograph taken in 2006 *by the author looking north on Main Street and taken from just south of the intersection of Fourth Street. The Lutheran Church to right center once had a tall steeple similar to the Presbyterian Church across the street. The steeple was removed during the renovations of 1941. It had been hit by lightning three times in the past.*

51

The Watsontown Brick Company, *real photo postcard by Nelson Caulkins, circa 1917.*

Another real photo postcard *of the Watsontown Brick Company.*

Workers *at the Watsontown Brick Company. Real photo postcard, circa 1920.*

Bicentennial brick paperweight,
4" long, made by Glen-Gery Brick Company in 1976.

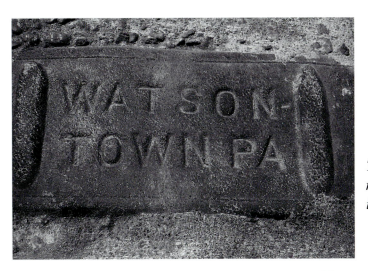

This Watsontown Brick Company brick, *marked "Watsontown, Pa.," is cemented in the author's sidewalk in Virginia.*

This Nelson Caulkins real photo postcard, circa 1917, shows the Pennsylvania Railroad just outside of Watsontown.

The south end of Watsontown showing the Pennsylvania Railroad Station. *Real photo postcard, circa 1910.*

The railroad at Watsontown, *an early postcard view. The photographer is facing north from the south end of town. In the distance is the overhead bridge at First Street over the PRR tracks.*

The PRR station *at Watsontown. On the left edge of the photo postcard is the watchman's shanty.*

55

Another early real photo postcard view of the railroad station at Watsontown.

The PRR tracks at Watsontown, a real photo postcard view looking north. To the right is *Pennsylvania Avenue.*

This view *of Pennsylvania Avenue includes a PRR steam train. Real photo postcard, postmarked 1909.*

1970s: The Watsontown train station *as it appeared circa 1977. Photograph by the author.*

An exceptional photo postcard view *of the Lewisburg, Milton, and Watsontown Passenger Railway Company trolley. The trolley was active from 1898 to 1928.*

The photographer's identification *(on the tree) of this postcard, "Main St., Looking south, Watsontown, Pa." This was taken from the corner of West Fifth and Main Streets, circa 1907. The church steeples at Fourth Street are in the distance.*

Facing south, *this view of the trolley also includes Klapp's Drug Store, opened in 1911, on the southeast corner of Main Street and Second Street (Brimmer Avenue). Caulkins real photo postcard, circa 1918.*

The Empire Restaurant *was located on the east side of Main Street, between Second Street (Brimmer Avenue) and First Street. The restaurant building was replaced in 1946 by the present building that held Becker's Ben Franklin Store during much of the second half of the twentieth century. Real photo postcard, circa 1907.*

59

A work crew repairing trolley tracks at the Watsontown Park. Real photo postcard, circa 1910.

Trolley conductors of the Lewisburg, Milton, and Watsontown Railway Company. Real photo postcard, circa 1915.

The Jr. Order of the United American Mechanics was founded in 1853 as a nativist, pro American organization. By 1930 it grew to over 2,900 councils. Watsontown's council was #514. Though the Jr. O.U.A.M. symbol resembles the Masonic symbol, the two organizations held no relationship.

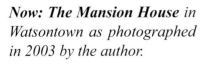

A real photo view of Main Street, Watsontown, circa 1915. Along the right margin of the postcard are Klapp's Drug Store and Berger's Stationery Store.

Now: The Mansion House in Watsontown as photographed in 2003 by the author.

Real photo postcard of the former borough building in Watsontown, circa 1916, located on the corner of Fourth and Main Streets. The building was bought by Watsontown Borough in 1912 and used to house the West Branch Fire Company as well as a municipal building. It was razed to make way for the present borough building built during 1960 - 1961.

Odd Fellows lodge ribbon from Watsontown Lodge No. 619

The borough building or "Town Hall" as labeled on this postcard by photographer Nelson Caulkins, circa 1917. In 1913 a group which formed the Watsontown Civic Club began raising funds for the clock and clock tower shown in this view. The sign on the third floor window indicates that the IOOF (Odd Fellows) lodge met there.

62

Then: The Town Hall or borough building after it was painted in 1938.

Now: The Watsontown Borough Building as photographed in 2006 by the author. The present building is located on the site of the former municipal building.

63

The Watsontown School at Eighth and Elm Streets as it appeared in 1907. The school, built in 1882, served all grades until 1924. It became a grammar school when the high school on Second Street (Brimmer Avenue) was completed. Real photo postcard.

A winter view of Watsontown School on Eighth Street, circa 1938. This photo postcard is addressed on the reverse side to Willis Fuller, brother of postcard photographer Ralph Fuller. This postcard, however, is not a Fuller postcard.

*Labeled **"Grammar School,"** this photo postcard of the Eighth Street school was taken after the high school on Second Street (Brimmer Avenue) was opened in 1924.*

*The **Watsontown High School** on Brimmer Avenue and Canal Street, circa 1940. Finished in 1924, the first graduating class was the class of 1925. Real photo postcard.*

Harvest displays on church altars *were popular in the first part of the twentieth century. This remarkable Deininger photo postcard depicts "Harvest Home" in October 1919 at the First Lutheran Church of Watsontown.*

Watsontown's Roll of Honor, *located at the old borough building, displayed the names of Watsontown's WWI veterans, including six honored dead. Real photo postcard, circa 1920.*

The Watsontown Table and Furniture Company *along the railroad at Watsontown. This company was sold to Philco Corporation in 1936. Real photo postcard.*

WATSONTOWN CABINET CO. PLANT WATSONTOWN, PA. 587-3

The Watsontown Cabinet Company *was formed in 1936 by Philco Corporation. It had originally been the Watsontown Table and Furniture Company. The next year Philco also acquired the Watsontown Door and Sash Company and integrated it into its cabinet company. Real photo postcard.*

Cast iron dog paperweights advertising Bucki Carbon & Ribbons. These were made at the Watsontown Foundry.

Cast iron miniature bean pot made at Watsontown Foundry.

THE GEM THEATRE
SPECIAL TO-NIGHT
WEDNESDAY, FEBRUARY 28th

Come and See LILLIAN WALKER in "GREEN STOCKINGS." The famous stage success. Vitagraph Blue Ribbon in 5-parts. Also, Comedy.

THURSDAY, March 1st—Franks Mills in "THE HOUSE OF MIRRORS" in 5 parts. Also, Comedy. Mutual film.

FRIDAY—Edwin Arden in "THE GRAY MASK" 5-parts. Also, 9th Chapter of HELEN HOLMES.

SATURDAY—Matinee 2:30—The World Famous Star, Nat Goodwin in "A WALL STREET TRAGEDY" in 5-parts. Also· Comedy.

MONDAY, 5th—Pearl White in "THE IRON CLAW"

Playbill for the Gem Theatre in Watsontown. The Gem Theatre operated in the early twentieth century.

Published postcard of the Gem Theatre. The Gem was located where the Watson Theatre now stands.

Then: ***This photo postcard*** *of the Watson Theatre at 131 Main Street was taken in the 1940s. The original building, once known as the Gem Theatre and later the Lyceum Theatre, burned in 1934 and was rebuilt in 1940 as the Watson Theatre.*

Now: ***The Watson Theatre*** *continues to show movies to the present day. Photo by the author, 2006.*

The Watsontown National Bank *as photographed by Nelson Caulkins, circa 1917. Real photo postcard.*

Front entrance *to the Watsontown National Bank. This real photo postcard appears to have been taken in the 1920s.*

The Watsontown National Bank on the corner of Main Street and Third Street, Watsontown. This real photo postcard is from the 1940s.

The Methodist Church on Third Street in Watsontown was completed in 1872. Real photo postcard, circa 1908.

This early 1900s real photo postcard depicts a late colonial era limestone house near Watsontown.

Early Watsontown area postcard, labeled "I.F. Saul residence."

Brick house, home of Elmer Winter. Real photo postcard, circa 1910.

Early postcard depicting a frame house at the corner of Ash and Sixth Streets. This house, 515 Ash Street, still stands.

Early postcard of a house located at 501 Elm Street.

Three of these Watsontown houses in this early postcard are identified: Top left, 501 Elm Street, top right, 419 Elm Street, bottom left, 401 Elm Street.

Early postcard *of a house in Watsontown.*

A Watsontown home. *Real photo postcard, circa 1920.*

House of William F. Shay *at 510 Main Street, Watsontown. Real photo postcard, circa 1910. Shay, Chief Burgess of Watsontown in the early 1900s, was the great grandson of Samuel Wallis of Muncy Farms near Halls Station. During the Revolutionary War, Wallis, who had built an empire from land transactions, pretended to be a patriot but was really a British spy. Much later, during the twentieth century, the Shay house in Watsontown was owned by William Wagner Cronrath and has become known to area residents as the Cronrath house.*

This Caulkins photo postcard*, circa 1918, shows the Fred Rombach house at 1002 North Main Street. Rombach was instrumental in the growth of Philco's cabinet division in Watsontown in the 1930s. This house looks nearly the same today.*

*A **house*** *in Watsontown, circa 1910. Real photo postcard.*

*A **blacksmith shop*** *in Watsontown. Real photo postcard, circa 1907.*

This real photo postcard, *"Home of Wertman, Watsontown, Pa.," is postmarked December 10, 1906.*

The William Sechler house *at 1006 Elm Street, real photo postcard, circa 1910.*

A postcard of the borough building decorated with American flags, 1915.

An Old Home Week pin, 1915.

Watsontown Boot & Shoe Company token made for Old Home Week, 1915.

A photo postcard of the Mansion House decorated with American flags, circa 1915.

A Watsontown house, circa 1915, decorated with American flags. Real photo postcard.

A 1915 photo postcard of Main Street decorated with American flags. At right center is the First Lutheran Church.

A group of Watsontown people at 205 Main Street awaiting a parade, circa 1915. The right side of this postcard shows a restaurant at 207 Main Street, now the Hendershot Photography Studio.

OLD HOME WEEK
WATSONTOWN

Six Days, Commencing

Monday, August 23

JOHNNY J. JONES EXPOSITION SHOWS

5 BIG FREE ACTS 5

50 ATTRACTIONS 50

Undivided, Just as It Appeared in all the Large Cities

Ash St. Park. 5th and 6th Sts.

OFFICIAL PROGRAM

WATSONTOWN

OLD HOME WEEK

AUGUST 22=28, 1915

WATSONTOWN, PA.

Program of Events

Sunday, August 22

10:30 a. m.—Special services in all churches; sermon by former pastors.

5:00 p. m.—Parade of Sunday Schools; Sons of Veterans Reserves escort to Watsontown Park. Short addresses; music by the bands and large chorus choir.

All Sunday Schools and Congregations will form in line at their respective Houses of Worship at 5:00 p.m. The Executive Committee will meet at City Hall and head the parade. The M. E. School, led by Housel's Watsontown Band, will march up Main street followed by the Lutheran and Presbyterian schools. At Fifth and Main Trate's Military Band will swing into line, followed by the Baptist and Reformed schools. At Ninth street, the Third Regiment, Sons of Veterans Reserves, headed by the 3rd Regiment Band, followed by the Sunday Schools, will proceed to Watsontown Park.

Monday, August 23

12:01 a. m.—Formal opening of Old Home Week celebration at the Municipal building. Address by Chairman of the Executive Committee.

Incoming of guests during the day.

8:00 p. m.—Band Concert.

Tuesday, August 24

2:00 p. m.—Formal reception and welcome in Watsontown Park.

8:00 p. m.—Crowning of Queen of Old Home Week in Court of Honor at Fourth and Main streets. Band concert.

Wednesday, August 25
Civic Parade, 2:00 p. m.

First Division

Chief Marshal, D. F. Wagner. Aides, Captain A. K. Batdorf and Samuel High.

Co. C, N. G. P., Milton.
Col. T. S. Morgan and staff.
Third Regiment, S. of V. Reserves Band.
Third Regiment, S. of V. Reserves.

Second Division

Chief Marshal, H. C. Krisher. Aide, M. S. Adams.

Queen float with escort.
I. O. O. F. Orphanage Band.
Civic Body, Fraternal Orders.

Third Division

Chief Marshal, W. C. Brimmer; Aide, M. Y. Leinbach.

Trate's Military Band.
Fraternal Orders and Floats; all other floats.

Fourth Division

Marshal, F. A. Reen; Aide, S. B. Morgan.

Housel's Watsontown Band.
Bryson Post, G.A.R., in automobiles.
Sunbury Business Men's Association.

Formation of Parade

Right of line, east side of Main street, above Fourth.

Second Division, Civic body, East Fourth street.

Third Division, floats, west side of Main street, above Fourth.

Queen's float to be at corner of Main and Fourth streets.

Fourth Division, West Fourth st.

Parade forms at 1:30, moves at two o'clock.

Route—Down Main to station, to Pennsylvania avenue, to Third, to Liberty, to Eighth, to Ash, to Fourth, to Elm, to Tenth, to Main, down Main to station. Countermarch to City Hall.

3.00 p. m.—Ball Game. Athletic Park. Milton vs Watsontown.

8:00 p. m.—Band Concert.

Thursday, August 26

Public School and Children's parade, 3:00 p. m.

All pupils of schools; all children under six years of age and babies in decorated coaches.

I. O. O. F. Orphanage Band, Housel's Watsontown Band, and Trate's Military Band.

Parade will form at public school house on Eighth street. Down Main to station. Countermarch to City Hall.

4:00 p. m.—Ball Game. Muncy vs Watsontown.

8:00 p. m.—Automobile parade.

9:00 p. m.—Band Concert.

Friday, August 27

Industrial and Farmers' Parade, at 3:00 p. m.

Chief Marshal and Aides.

First Division. Montgomery Band. Montgomery-Watsontown Assn.

Second Division

Trate's Military Band.
Industrial and Farmers' Display.

Program of Events

Third Division

Housel's Watsontown Band.
Industrial and Farmers' Display.

Parade will form on Fourth street, East and West.

Same route as Civic Parade.

4:00 p. m.—Baseball game. Montgomery vs Watsontown.

Mummers' Carnival, 8:00 p. m.

First Division. Housel's Watsontown Band.

Second Division. Montgomery Band.

Third Division. Trate's Military Band.

Parade will form on Fourth street, East and West. Up Elm to Tenth, to Main, down Main to station. Countermarch to City Hall.

9:00 p. m.—Band Concert.

Saturday, August 28

Firemen's Parade, 2:30 p. m.
State Constabulary.

Marshal, W. A. Nicely; Aide, D. F. Wagner.

First Division

Sunbury Fire Dept., Chief Stroh and assistants.

Gaskin's Military Band.

Good Intent Co., No. 1 Steam Fire Co.; Washington Steam Fire Co.; Rescue Hose Co.; Americus Hose Co.; Band. Friendship Hose Co.; East End Hose Co.; Good Will Hose Co.

Second Division

Aides, M. Y. Leinbach, R. M. Moore.
Housel's Watsontown Band.
Miltonian Fire Co., Milton.
Shimer Hose Co., Milton.
Fifth Ward Hose Co., Milton.
Good Will Hose Co., Milton.
Independent Fire Co., Milton.
Northumberland Fire Co.

Third Division

Aides: M. S. Adams, W. B. Russell.
Renovo Band.
Renovo Fire Department.
Wm. Cameron Engine Co., Lewisburg.
Willing Hand Hose Co., Montoursville.
Millville Fire Co., Millville.
Mifflinburg Fire Co., Mifflinburg.

Fourth Division

Aides: Geo. B. Sterner, L. M. Wesner.
Trate's Military Band.
Dewart Fire Company.

West Branch Volunteer Fire Co., No. 1, of Watsontown.

FORMATION—First Division. Sunbury Department, Main street, between Fourth and Sixth. Second Division, Milton, on West Sixth street; Northumberland on East Sixth street. Third Division, Renovo, Lewisburg and Montoursville on West Fifth st.; Millville and Mifflinburg on East 5th st. Fourth Division, Dewart on West Fourth st., Watsontown on East 4th street.

Route—Same as Civic Parade.

3:30 p. m.—Ball Game. Sunbury vs Watsontown.

8:00 p. m.—Band Concert.

OLD HOME WEEK PRIZES

Civic Parade

Best float in line—$10.00.
Second best float—bevel-edge mirror.

School and Children's Parade

Grade making best appearance—$5
Second best appearance—picture and frame.

Best appearing baby coach—$5.00.
Second best baby coach—oak rocker.
Third best baby coach—counterpane.

Automobile Parade

Best decorated automobile—$10.00.
Second best—electric auto horn.
Third best—5 gallons Polarine oil.

Industrial and Farmers' Parade

Best float in line—$10.00.
Second best—carving set.
Third best—pair footstools.
Best farmer's exhibit in line—$10.
Second best—safety razor.

Mummers' Carnival

Best mummers' band in line—$10.
Most comical float in line—$5.00.
Most comical ladies' costume—Cameo ring.

Most comical gent's costume—silk shirt.

Finest ladies' costume—5-pound box candy.

Finest gent's costume—pencil sharpener.

Firemen's Parade

Tallest fireman in line—pipe.
Shortest adult fireman in line—ash tray.

Heaviest fireman in line—fountain pen.

Old Home Week program, August, 1915.

*A **House decorated with flags,*** *real photo postcard, circa 1910. This house is on the northwest corner of Main Street and the alley between Fifth and Fourth Streets (across Main Street from the Blue Diamond restaurant of the 1950s).*

Beatrice Cronrath *with her baby in a decorated baby carriage. Real photo postcard, circa 1911.*

The Dewart Creamery truck in the Industrial Parade for Watsontown's Old Home Week. Real photo postcard, taken August 27, 1915.

"It pays to wear Watsontown Shoes," claims the banner on the back of this touring car in a Watsontown parade. The Watsontown Boot and Shoe Company ceased production in 1927. Real photo postcard.

The Quick Lunch wagon *of C.E. Blair. Real photo postcard, circa 1915.*

Horse-drawn wagon *decorated in beautiful patriotic regalia. Real photo postcard, circa 1910.*

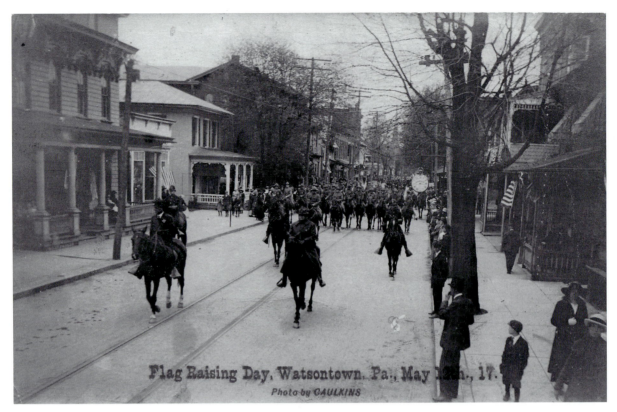

A Nelson Caulkins photo postcard of the parade in Watsontown on Flag Raising Day, May 12, 1917. This photo was taken at the south end of Main Street facing north. To the left of the big tree is the famous pocket watch style clock which once stood in front of the Empire Restaurant.

Another Caulkins photo postcard *of the parade on Flag Raising Day in Watsontown.*

Crowd at Flag Raising Day in Watsontown, 1917. A Nelson Caulkins photo postcard.

A crowd after the parade includes Boy Scouts and Red Cross nurses. Caulkins real photo postcard, 1917.

Within image: Flag Raising Day, Watsontown, Pa., May 12th., 17.
Photo by CAULKINS

Caulkins postcard of the Red Cross ladies *in the parade on Flag Raising Day, May 12, 1917. Notice how barren the trees are in mid May, 1917.*

Within image: WATSONTOWN, PA. JULY 4TH 18.   CAULKINS

Unusual double view postcard *of the Red Cross nurses in the Watsontown July 4, 1918 parade. The parade was part of the American Red Cross carnival held on Independence Day. The lower photo shows the McEwensville Red Cross ladies. At the time of this parade, over 3,600,000 Americans were members of the American Red Cross. A 1918 reference book on the Great War stated, "The Red Cross, as a volunteer organization offers a fitting medium through which the volunteer spirit of the country may exert itself in war. That volunteer spirit is a very precious asset and it should be guided and directed exclusively as a volunteer effort with enthusiasm, lack of red tape, and unlimited opportunity...Some such medium as the Red Cross, unofficial and unmarshalled by the formal process of government, is absolutely necessary to mobilize effectively the human, the humane, and imaginative qualities necessary in alleviating the suffering so inevitable in war.* (10)*"*

*A **Red Cross** parade vehicle* at Watsontown. Real photo postcard, circa 1918.

*A **double view** postcard* depicting Caulkins photographs of the Watsontown July 4, 1918 parade held during the Red Cross Carnival.

A remarkable real photo postcard by Nelson Caulkins of the Camp Fire Girls in the July 4, 1918 parade in Watsontown. *The Camp Fire Girls originated in 1910 and was the sister organization of the Boys Scouts of America. On the float is written the Camp Fire Law, "Seek Beauty, Give Service, Pursue Knowledge, Be Trustworthy, Hold on to Health, Glorify Work, Be Happy." Camp Fire Girls were never required to take the oath or recite the law. It was an unspoken code by which to live. One of the founders of the Camp Fire Girls, Luther Gulick said of the law, "The power of the law is within you. It is not law that other people can demand you obey, that is, it is not law from without – it is law from the heart. It commands only those who seek to follow. It is opportunity, not obligation. It is an open road leading to the beautiful country where you live, rather than chains which would bind or limit your freedom.* (11)"

The origins of the Camp Fire Girls are complex and involve a number of people. A few individuals, though, from the very beginnings of the organization, were instrumental in the American Indian theme and influence: In 1910, Dr. Gulick's wife, Charlotte Vetter Gulick, started a girls' camp with an Indian theme, called WoHeLo, from the words, work, health and love. Charlotte Vetter got the idea of the Indian theme from renown author Ernest Thompson Seton and his wife Julia, who also wrote Indian lore books. Ernest Thompson Seton was instrumental in helping to establish the Boy Scouts of America and Camp Fire Girls. A relatively unknown contributor was Dr. Charles A. Eastman, a Native American medical doctor who knew the Setons and worked for the YMCA. The YMCA was a youth organization which helped to establish the Boy Scouts of America. Eastman wrote a book in 1914 entitled, "Indian Scout Talks, A Guide for Boy Scouts and Camp Fire Girls." By 1918 when the Caulkins photograph was taken, the American Indian theme was an integral part of the Camp Fire Girls. (12)

The Italy booth at the Red Cross Carnival in Watsontown, July 4, 1918. Caulkins real photo postcard.

Boy Scout Troop 9 of Selinsgrove in Watsontown for the July 4, 1918 parade. Caulkins real photo postcard.

Arch in Watsontown *erected for the Welcome Home Celebration of July 4 & 5, 1919. Caulkins photo postcard.*

The Watsontown Table and Furniture Company, *July 4, 1919. This is a rare early Deininger photo postcard.*

The July 4th festivities of 1919 included a welcome home celebration for the WWI veterans returning from overseas. This truck was entered by Watsontown Door and Sash Company. Caulkins photo postcard.

Men of the Watsontown Brick Company are decked out in patriotic regalia for the July 4, 1919 Welcome Home Celebration. Real photo postcard.

Joe Burkhart and his dog. Real photo postcard, early 1900s.

A goat-pulled child's sulky in Watsontown. Real photo postcard.

An aerial view of Watsontown, circa 1939. A computerized zoom of this photo postcard shows the two spires of the churches on Fourth and Main Streets. The Lutheran church spire was removed during the renovations of 1940 – 41. It also shows the municipal or borough building after it was painted in 1938. Thus, this photo must have been taken between late 1938 and 1941.

94

William Wagner Cronrath, *age 12, in the buggy on Elm Street. Real photo postcard, circa 1921.*

Ira Aldrich and his wife, circa 1910.

Real photo postcard of unknown location, circa 1919. From the Koch - Cronrath family photo archives.

Two WWI era soldiers. The one on the left is Oliver Koch of Watsontown, who was the father of Marjorie Louise Koch Cronrath. Real photo postcard, circa 1919.

The West Branch Fire Company of Watsontown. This postcard, postmarked June 25, 1907, shows the Silsby Steam Fire Engine, a classic Victorian fire apparatus destroyed by fire in 1925 at the C.F. Sheffer plant in Dewart. The firemen are: Myerly, Foresman, Wesner, Ulrich, Wagner, Wertman, Watts, Raup, Nicely, Wertman, and Muffly. There are two known poses of this photo session.

Labeled "Watsontown firemen," this postcard shows circa 1900 fire equipment. Real photo postcard.

Trate's Third Regiment Band *of Watsontown. Charles E. Trate had a music store at 225 Main Street, Watsontown (later the opera house) and organized the Third Regiment Band of the Sons of Veteran Reserves. Eventually the band was incorporated into the 12th Regiment of the Pennsylvania National Guard. Trate died at the young age of 45, but the band continued on for several years after his death. Real photo postcard.*

Trate's Third Regiment Band *at Camp Ripple, Scranton, Pa. Real photo postcard.*

Trate's Band at Gettysburg, Pa. *The drum, now marked 12th Regiment Band, shows that this photo postcard by W.H. Tipton of Gettysburg, was taken after the band was inducted into the Pennsylvania National Guard. The band marched with distinction at the Gettysburg encampments. This photo was likely taken at the 1913 reunion at Gettysburg, a grand encampment of thousands of veterans commemorating the 50th anniversary of the battle. Tipton took many of the professional photographs of the encampment for the book, "Fiftieth Anniversary of the Battle of Gettysburg, Report of the Pennsylvania Commission, December 31, 1913."*

Housel's Band *emerged from the Old Cornet Band, first organized in 1872. Housel's Band was directed by Dr. Joseph R. Housel, a Watsontown dentist who had served in the Civil War. Housel was considered to be a talented musician.*

Cabinet Photograph: This is a rare Caulkins photograph of the Girls Scouts at Watsontown, circa *1918. At left center in white shoes is Thelma Caulkins, Nelson Caulkins' daughter. Front row, left to right: Unidentified girl, Mabel Sterner, unidentified girl, Thelma Caulkins, Helen Ester McFarland (holding the flag), Margaret Rombach, Helen Thornton, Kathryn Klingman, Ruth McFarland. Back row, left to right: Kathryn Weil, Peg Barr, Lena Vannstrand, Elizabeth Royer, Alberta Aunkst, Phyllis Ungard, Elda McCormick. Photograph formerly owned and submitted by Harry Carson.*

Trate's business card for his music store.

The seventh grade at Watsontown School. *Photo postcard taken by Nelson Caulkins, October 27, 1919. In the back row, fourth from left (head at corner of window ledge) is Nelson Caulkins' son, Frank. The teacher that year was Miss Anna McCormick.*

An early photo postcard *of the first and second grades at Watsontown. The teacher is Maude Williams.*

Class of 1909, *Watsontown. This photo postcard view was taken of the students as they stood on the front porch of the Watsontown School at Eighth Street. Real photo postcard.*

Class of 1910, *Watsontown, on the porch of the Watsontown School. Real photo postcard.*

Class of 1911, *Watsontown, taken at the school on Eighth Street. Real photo postcard.*

Senior Class of 1912 *at Watsontown. Front row, left to right, Margaret Marsh, Frances Wagner Hastings, Helen Lewis, Ruth Sechler, Mollie Myerly, Clyde Metzger. Back row, left to right, Ralph Dawson, Sara McFarland, Banks Smith, John Cooner, Professor Martin, Bessie Waltman Armstrong.*

Junior Class of 1912 at Watsontown. Real photo postcard.

Another pose of the Junior Class of 1912 at Watsontown. Real photo postcard.

Sophomore Class of 1912 at Watsontown High School. *Real photo postcard.*

Freshman Class of 1912 at Watsontown High School. *Real photo postcard.*

An unidentified theater group in Watsontown, *circa early 1900s. Real photo postcard.*

Watsontown baseball team *of 1909. Real photo postcard.*

A family portrait taken at the Cronrath home at 19 Second Street (later Brimmer Avenue) in September of 1913. Front row, left to right, Sylvia Carpenter Cronrath (1833-1916), Mercy Myerly (1841-1922), Helen Cronrath Aunkst (1911-1999), Jeremiah Myerly (1845-1921) holding Paul E. Cronrath (1913-1998), William Wagner Cronrath (1909-1995), Katherine Wolfe, Elmira Wagner (1849-1927).

Back row, left to right, William Carpenter Cronrath (1863-1938), Fannie Wolfe Cronrath (1864-1937), Herman S. Cronrath (1891-1975), Beatrice Myerly Cronrath (1891-1967), Clara Myerly (1871-1943), Simon Myerly (1866-1921). Real photo postcard.

Beatrice Cronrath holding her daughter Helen. Beside her is her son William Wagner Cronrath. Real photo postcard, late summer, 1911.

The children of Herman and Beatrice Cronrath of Watsontown. In the back row are Helen and William and in front is Paul. Real photo postcard, circa 1915.

The baby in the bowl is Katherine Wertman Moltz of Second Street (Brimmer Avenue), Watsontown. Mrs. Moltz taught sixth grade at the Watsontown School on Eighth Street. Real photo postcard, circa early 1900s.

William Wagner Cronrath. Real photo postcard, circa 1915.

Oliver Sanders Koch and Ruth Pauline Sechler Koch *in a studio portrait which used a fake car prop. Real photo postcard, early 1900s.*

Alice Barber Moyer, *in the center of the postcard, holding a folding camera. Real photo postcard, circa early 1920s.*

Photo postcard *of the female workers of L.A. Lindauer, Custom Tailor, taken July 4, 1911.*

Photo postcard *of the employees of L.A. Lindauer, July 4, 1911.*

Men dressed as women, *women as men, circa 1915, in this comic get-up for Halloween. Real photo postcard.*

Watsontown Door and Sash Company *employees photographed by Lester Deininger in 1916. Real photo postcard.*

1910 Calendar of the Watsontown Door & Sash Company. *This company was bought by Philco Corporation in 1937.*

Martin's Susquehanna Eight jazz band. Real photo postcard.

Another view of Martin's Susquehanna Eight. Real photo postcard.

Along the Susquehanna River near Watsontown.
Real photo postcard, circa 1910.

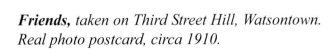

Friends, taken on Third Street Hill, Watsontown.
Real photo postcard, circa 1910.

First Boy Scout troop *in Watsontown as photographed in 1911. The Boy Scouts were started in America in 1910.*

Photograph of the Watsontown Boy Scout troop *on a hike near White Deer in 1912.*

Watsontown Boy Scout Troop 610 *in 1974, a very late period real photo postcard. The author's nephew, Jim Lehman is in the back row, third from the right.*

Boy Scout Troop 610 *on its way to a camping trip. Real photo postcard, 1974.*

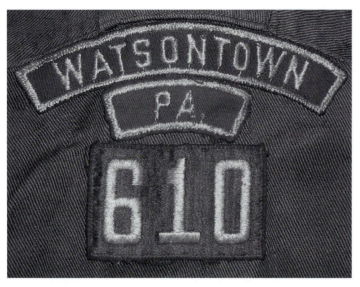

Boy Scout patches *on a shirt from Watsontown Troop 610, circa 1964.*

The author's Eagle Scout award *from Watsontown Troop 610, circa 1966.*

Order of the Arrow *patch for the Wapsu Achtu Lodge as worn by the author as a member of Watsontown Troop 610, circa 1965.*

Two BSA rank insignia *and three patrol insignia from Watsontown Troop 610, circa 1964.*

Entrance to the Watsontown Memorial Park, *often referred to as Watsontown Park, circa 1910. In front of the entrance is the trolley track. Real photo postcard.*

Watsontown Park *just south of town. Real photo postcard, circa 1940. Restrooms, bleachers, and dugouts were built in 1936 with WPA assistance.*

Riverside Park, *south of Watsontown on the road to Milton. The trolley is seen on the left. Real photo postcard, circa 1910.*

Riverside Park, *along the Susquehanna River south of Watsontown, circa 1907. The photographer for this real photo postcard is Fosnot. Lew Fosnot owned the Watsontown Record and Star newspaper. His son, John Clyde Fosnot was in the printing business with him.*

One of the pavilions in Riverside Park, circa 1907. This postcard view was taken by John Wilson of Milton. Wilson was a professional portrait photographer with studios in Milton and Washingtonville. He was also responsible for many outstanding real photo postcards of those two areas.

A real photo postcard view of Riverside Park, circa 1910. Wilson real photo postcard.

*A **view** of Riverside Park, circa 1907. This postcard is labeled "Milton, Pa." because the park was located between Watsontown and Milton. This card was marketed as a Milton souvenir postcard by John Wilson of Milton.*

*A **view** of the swings at Riverside Park, circa 1907. This is a Fosnot real photo postcard.*

The trolley at Riverside Park. This real photo postcard view labeled "Milton Park," was taken by John Wilson, a Milton photographer, circa 1907.

A real photo postcard view of Riverside Park, circa 1912. To the left is Diehl's Bakery Wagon.

A Wilson postcard view of the river, circa 1907.

One of the worst floods to hit the Susquehanna Valley was the Flood of '36. Shown in this real photo postcard is a fruit stand between Milton and Watsontown, March 18 or 19, 1936.

A Caulkins photo postcard of the Susquehanna River at Watsontown, circa 1918.

Looking north up the Susquehanna from Watsontown. Real photo postcard.

Bly's Ferry at Watsontown, still in use in the early twentieth century. At the time this photo postcard was made, the ferry was owned by David L. Bly. Its use was discontinued in 1928 after the White Deer - Watsontown bridge was opened.

Two metal buttons found at the Bly Ferry House site by the author in the early 1970s.

A dog in the river at Watsontown, circa 1920. Real photo postcard.

Flood waters near Watsontown. *Early twentieth century, real photo postcard.*

The White Deer – Watsontown bridge replaced the ferry at Watsontown in 1928. *Real photo postcard, circa1940.*

The Susquehanna River *at Watsontown after the bridge was built in 1928. Real photo postcard, circa 1940.*

The Susquehanna, *showing the White Deer - Watsontown bridge. Real photo postcard.*

The towpath for the Pennsylvania Canal at Watsontown. The canal continued in use into the early twentieth century. Real photo postcard.

The Port May locks of the Pennsylvania Canal south of Watsontown. Real photo postcard, early twentieth century.

The Port May locks below Watsontown after they had fallen into disrepair. Real photo postcard.

Early flat buttons found along the canal north of Watsontown.

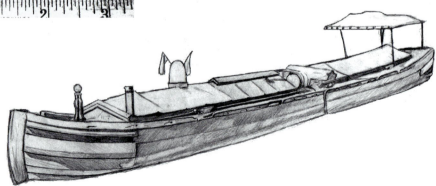

Robert McClure sketch of a canal boat.

CHAPTER 3
McEWENSVILLE

In the first quarter of the nineteenth century, two miles up stream from the mouth of the Warrior Run, a village developed called Pine Grove. In 1825 Adam Sarver sold a number of lots anticipating a growth of population. Because there was another Pine Grove in Pennsylvania, it was decided to change the name of the growing community to avoid confusion. (1)

On October 25, 1825, Captain Alexander McEwen, a Scotsman, a weaver, veteran of the War of 1812, and owner of a store and inn in Pine Grove, was hosting a dinner party for the line officers and guests of nearby Camp Calhoun. Guests at the dinner party included the field officers of the Independent Battalion of Volunteers; Brigadier General Adam Dougal, Brigadier General Light, Major John Montgomery, Major Robert Hammond, Captain Henry Frick of the Milton Guards, Captain William Fulkerson of the Warrior Run Infan-

try, Captain Jackson McFadden of the Lewisburg Guards, Captain James Finney of the Union Guards, and Captain John Ludwig of the Lafayette Artillerists, among others. During conversation the topic arose of the newly planned community and the fact that no one had yet derived a name. Brigadier General Light proposed a toast, "May we shortly have the satisfaction of seeing a new and flourishing village, situated in the immediate vicinity of Camp Calhoun and may it be appropriately named McEwensville (2)."

Thus began McEwensville, a quiet but busy farming community located between Watsontown and Turbotville in Northumberland County. McEwensville was part of Turbot Township until April 15, 1843 when by decree of court Delaware Township was formed. From then until November 7, 1857, McEwensville was part of Delaware Township. On that date by decree of court,

McEwensville, *a Ralph Fuller real photo postcard, circa 1908.*

McEwensville was incorporated as an independent borough. Watsontown and McEwensville remained through the nineteenth and twentieth centuries, the only boroughs surrounded by Delaware Township.

During the 1800s there were five churches in McEwensville; Lutheran, Reformed, Baptist, Methodist, and Presbyterian. The Lutheran church and Reformed church (now United Church of Christ) are the only ones to survive to the twenty-first century. In 1842 the Lutheran and Reformed congregations built a church on Green Street (now Church Street), but in 1873 the Lutherans purchased the interest of the Reformed congregation. The Reformed congregation then built a two story brick structure at the corner of Main Street and Route 44 (the road to Turbotville). The Methodist church was built in 1867 but became defunct by turn of the century and was bought by the borough to be used as a town hall. The Presbyterian church was organized in 1842, but disbanded just after 1900. The Baptist church fell into ruin by turn of

the century and was torn down. (3)

In 1852 a brick academy, a private subscription school, was built on David Gold's land near the cemetery in McEwensville (4). In 1871 the use of the building was transferred to the local school board and from that date to 1958 served as a public school. Until 1921 it was used for all grades. From then until 1949, McEwensville school served first through eighth grades. High school students could choose between Milton, Watsontown, and Turbotville. From 1949 through 1958, seventh and eighth grades attended other schools in the Turbotville area. During World War II one of the teachers at the McEwensville school was Neoska Fuller, daughter of postcard photographer Ralph Fuller. Neoska told how her students rushed to the windows to watch a convoy of military trucks pass through town (5). In recent years the building served as a firehouse for the McEwensville Volunteer Fire Department. Today the building is vacant.

Throughout the nineteenth century several busi-

James Bannen Swope real photo postcard of McEwensville, postmarked 1908.

nesses related to wagon and carriage building thrived in McEwensville. Around mid century a newspaper, the West Branch Intelligencer was published. A man named Trapp carried on a daguerreotype studio from his wagon. In town were a lawyer's office, a doctor's office, a dentist's office, two foundries, a general store, and a combination drug store and grocery store. (6)

In 1886 the Wilkes Barre and Western Railroad was built from Watsontown to Millville, passing by the north end of McEwensville where a station was built. By the time the postcard photographers were in town in the early 1900s, this railroad was called the Susquehanna, Bloomsburg, and Berwick Railroad. In 1918, it became a branch of the Pennsylvania Railroad.

In 1908, during the height of the real photo postcard era, McEwensville had a population of just under 200. Recently, the population was listed as 273. A hundred years have not added immensely to McEwensville's growth. Many of the old, historic buildings still stand. The entrance to the "brick road" from McEwensville to Watsontown was changed in the 1960s, otherwise there have been few significant changes.

Now: Main Street, McEwensville. Photo taken by the author in 2003. Some of these buildings date to the early 1800s.

A very early US bridle rosette. This was made of stamped sheet brass with lead-fill in the back. It was found in McEwensville in the early 1970s and may be associated with Alexander McEwen's Camp Calhoun.

131

A bird's eye view of McEwensville. This Swope real photo postcard, circa 1908, was taken from a hilltop overlooking town.

"Looking from McEwensville to S.B. & B. RR. Station." This Ralph Fuller postcard was taken circa 1908. The S.B. & B. was the Susquehanna, Bloomsburg, and Berwick Railroad, which ran from Watsontown on the West Branch of the Susquehanna River, through Warrior Run and Turbotville, to Berwick on the North Branch of the Susquehanna River. A branch of the S.B. & B. also ran from Eyersgrove to Millville.

The SB&B at McEwensville. *Ralph Fuller postcard, circa 1908. The Susquehanna, Bloomsburg, and Berwick Railroad incorporated August 15, 1902. The railroad was formerly called the Central Pennsylvania and Western Railroad but that line was sold at foreclosure on March 10, 1902. It reorganized on July 31, 1902 as the S.B. & B. The S.B. & B. name was kept until April 15, 1918 when the line merged with the Pennsylvania Railroad. At the time that the 1972 Hurricane Agnes Flood caused substantial damage to the line, it was called the Watsontown Secondary Track of the Penn Central Railroad.* (7)

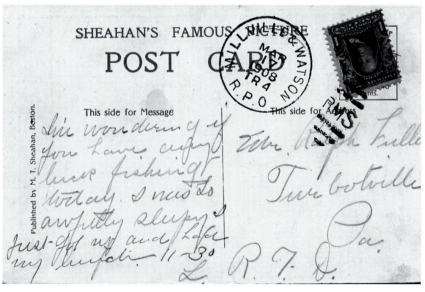

The back of a published postcard *sent to postcard photographer Ralph Fuller of Turbotville. This is an RPO cancellation (Railway Post Office) with the town names Millville & Watson(town) on the postmark. The TR4 represents Train # 4 and it is dated March 17, 1908 (St. Patrick's Day). This postmark means that the postcard was mailed, sorted, and postmarked on the mail car of the S.B.&B. The last RPO in the United States, where sorting and postmarking was actually done on the train, operated on June 30, 1977, between New York and Washington.*

133

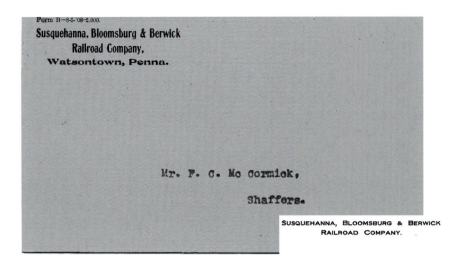

Form B—8-5-'08-2,000.

Susquehanna, Bloomsburg & Berwick
Railroad Company,
Watsontown, Penna.

Mr. F. C. Mc Cormick,

Shaffers.

Envelope and letter with the S.B.&B.
letterhead sent from Watsontown.

SUSQUEHANNA, BLOOMSBURG & BERWICK
RAILROAD COMPANY.

Form

WATSONTOWN, PA., Oct 8th, 1908.

Mr. Wm. Dollman, Foreman,
Eyersgrove, Pa.,

Dear Sir:—

Arrange to have your men unload car # 605 loaded with Yellow
Pine on top of hill at Paper Mill switch tomorrow morning. There are
some pieces not cut full to size, these pieces you will unload on a
separate pile from those cut full to size. Mr. Mc Cormick will designate
the pieces to be thrown out. Car will be placed by train # 1.

Yours truly,

F. & P. A.

Susquehanna, Bloomsburg & Berwick Railroad

TIME TABLE NO. 17

In Effect 6.00 A. M., MONDAY, JULY 2, 1917.

EASTERN TIME

_____

SPECIAL INSTRUCTIONS

_____

NOTE—When a rule is referred to by number, unless
otherwise specified, it is a rule in the Book of Rules.

Employes whose duties are affected by this Time Table
must have with them while on duty a copy with all effec-
tive supplements properly inserted.

TRAIN RULES.

STANDARD TIME.

1. Standard clock is located in the P. R. R. ticket office,
Watsontown.

TIME TABLE.

Letters and Characters.

2. The following letters and characters indicate: Rule
6 is amplified accordingly.
F—Stop on signal to receive or discharge passengers.
S—Regular stop.

---

10   **WATSONTOWN TO BERWICK.**
EASTWARD.

STATIONS.	Distance from Watsontown	Distance between Stations	1st Class. 2 L.E. DAILY EX. SUN. P. M.	2nd Class. Freight. 22 L.E. DAILY EX. SUN. A. M.	2nd Class. Mixed 20 L.E. DAILY EX. SUN. A. M.
WATSONTOWN	0.0	0.0	S 6.30	7.15	10.40
TRUCKENMILLERS	1.6	1.6	F 6.35	7.21	
McEWENSVILLE	2.4	0.8	F 6.38	7.25	S 10.50
WARRIOR RUN	3.7	1.3	F 6.42		
TURBOTVILLE	6.0	2.3	S 6.47	7.38	S 11.10
SCHUYLER	8.0	2.0	S 6.51	7.45	S 11.20
OTTAWA	9.8	1.8	S 6.56	7.52	S 11.30
DIEFFENBACH	11.3	1.5	F 7.00		
STRAWBERRY RIDGE	12.6	1.3	S 7.03	8.00	S 11.43
DERRY	14.6	2.0	F 7.08		
JERSEYTOWN	16.8	2.2	S 7.13	8.23	S 12.08
EYERSGROVE JUNC.	20.2	3.4	7.23 / 7.40	8.38	12.23 / 1.50
MORDANSVILLE	22.0	1.8	F 7.45		
BUCKHORN	25.5	3.5	F 7.55	8.58	2.10
PAPER MILL	27.3	1.8	F 8.00	9.08	2.20 / 2.35
LIGHT STREET	28.3	1.0	F 8.04	9.12	2.40
SUMMIT PASS'G SIDING	29.8	1.5	F 8.08	9.20	2.50
CABIN RUN	30.8	1.0	F 8.10		
FOWLERSVILLE	33.9	3.1	F 8.18	9.38	3.08
DENNIS MILLS	34.6	0.7	F 8.21		
EVANSVILLE	35.5	0.9	F 8.24		
LA SALLE STREET	38.6	3.1	F 8.32		
BERWICK	39.2	0.6	S 8.35	9.55	3.26
			P. M. 2 AR.DAILY EX.SUN	A. M. 22 AR.DAILY EX.SUN.	P. M. 20 AR.DAILY EX SUN

Train No. 20 will be mixed service Watsontown to
Eyersgrove Jct., and freight service only Eyersgrove Jct. to
Berwick.

Pages from a 1917 Susquehanna, Bloomsburg, and Berwick Railroad Timetable. *Courtesy of a railroad
timetable collector.*

Main Street, McEwensville.   *Swope photo postcard, postmarked 1907.*

A Swope *real photo postcard of Main Street, McEwensville, circa 1909.*

Front Street, or Main Street, McEwensville. Early real photo postcard.

An early Swope real photo postcard of McEwensville, circa 1907. The Swope Bros. signature is on the tree to the left.

Green Street, McEwensville, *now called Church Street. Swope real photo postcard, postmarked 1907.*

McEwensville *in the early 1900s. Real photo postcard, postmarked 1908.*

A McEwensville view *taken by Ralph Fuller, postmarked 1916.*

Green Street, McEwensville. *Swope photo postcard, circa 1908.*

The Reformed Church at McEwensville, *now called the United Church of Christ, is located at the corner of Rt. 44 and Main Street. Ralph Fuller real photo postcard, postmarked, 1908.*

Another view *of the Reformed Church at McEwensville. Real photo postcard, circa 1910.*

*Then: **An early postcard view,** circa 1910, of the Reformed Church at McEwensville.*

*Now: **The United Church of Christ** (Reformed Church) at McEwensville. Photo taken by the author, 2002.*

Then: The McEwensville School next to the cemetery. *Real photo postcard, postmarked, 1907.*

Now: The McEwensville School in use by the McEwensville Volunteer Fire Company, as photographed in 2003 by the author. Today, the school building is abandoned.

141

*A **house*** *in McEwensville. Real photo postcard, circa 1910.*

*A **house and picket fence*** *in McEwensville. Real photo postcard, circa 1910.*

Cows *in a house yard at McEwensville. Real photo postcard.*

A real photo postcard of McEwensville, *postmarked September 11, 1909. The engine of the S.B.&B. broke down that day and left about 70 people waiting for repairs.*

Swope real photo postcard of the McEwensville baseball team, circa 1908.

An early real photo postcard of the McEwensville baseball team.

A group of workers near McEwensville. Real photo postcard.

A saw mill near McEwensville. Such rigs were portable and moved from one location to another. Real photo postcard, postmarked 1908.

A line of men photographed near McEwensville. Real photo postcard.

A real photo postcard of three children in front of the McEwensville School, circa 1908.

A group of people near McEwensville. Real photo postcard.

146

A family group and dog in front of the McEwensville School. *Real photo postcard, circa 1910.*

Real photo postcard dated 1914 of a group of students *at the McEwensville School.*

A group of male students at McEwensville. Real photo postcard.

A real photo postcard of McEwensville graduates.

Gold Reunion, Aug. 15, 1907.

The Golds of McEwensville are descendents of George Thomas Gold. The Golds of Turbotville are descendents of Henry Daniel Gold. These two men were brothers, sons of David Gold (1806 – 1876), a farmer buried in Union Cemetery near McEwensville. (8) This photo postcard, taken by James Bannen Swope in 1907, shows the Gold Reunion in front of the McEwensville School. James Bannen Swope later became a brother-in-law of Ellen Gold when she married his brother Hugh Swope. Hugh and Ellen are the author's grandparents. David Gold is the author's great, great, great grandfather.

GOLD REUNION

A real photo postcard of the Gold Reunion at McEwensville, circa 1908.

149

Railroad repair *on the Susquehanna, Bloomsburg, and Berwick Railroad near McEwensville. Fuller real photo postcard, circa 1915.*

Railroad repair *on the SB & B Railroad near McEwensville. Fuller real photo postcar circa 1915.*

This Ralph Fuller real photo postcard, *circa 1910, shows the Warrior Run near McEwensville.*

Another Fuller photo postcard *showing the Warrior Run near McEwensville, circa 1910.*

This James Bannen Swope photo postcard, *circa 1908, shows the Warrior Run near McEwensville.*

The Warrior Run after a hard rain. *Caulkins real photo postcard, circa 1918.*

The Watsontown Brick Road *ran from McEwensville to Watsontown and was literally paved with bricks. This series of Caulkins real photo postcards was taken between 1917 and 1919.*

Another Caulkins view *of the Brick Road.*

An automobile *on the Watsontown Brick Road. Caulkins real photo postcard.*

The Brick Road *along the lower Warrior Run near Watsontown. Caulkins real photo postcard.*

White fence and a neat pastoral setting line the Watsontown Brick Road. Caulkins real photo postcard.

Bicycles on the Brick Road near Watsontown. Caulkins real photo postcard.

Now: The Brick Road near Watsontown, 2006. Photograph by the author.

CHAPTER 4
DELAWARE TOWNSHIP

This view of East Main Street, Dewart, was taken by James Bannen Swope, circa 1908.

Delaware Township consists of about 30 square miles of rural country in upper Northumberland County. The township surrounds Watsontown on three sides. Both Watsontown and Delaware Township are bounded on the west side by the Susquehanna River. Delaware Township includes Dewart but not McEwensville, for McEwensville, though lying within the township, became a separate borough in 1857. Delaware Township is bounded on the north by Lycoming County, the east by Lewis Township and on the south by Turbot Township.

Though Delaware Township did not come into existence until decreed by the Northumberland County Court on April 15, 1843, the area was settled prior to the Revolutionary War. After the French and Indian War, land was given to officers of the First and Second Battalions of the Pennsylvania Regiment of Foot in exchange for their service during the war. Captain William Piper re-

ceived 609 acres on the east side of the Susquehanna River in the area that is now Dewart and the western fringe of Delaware Township. Piper built a house at what later became Dewart. In July, 1775, he received a visit from Reverand Philip Fithian, the itinerant Presbyterian minister who preached at the first Warrior Run Church located where Watsontown Park is now. (1)

Several grist mills were operated at this time on the Warrior Run about four miles up from the mouth at the Susquehanna. Two of these mills, owned by Jacob Freeland and Daniel Vincent, were less than a half mile from what would become the Delaware Township boundry. Just inside the township boundry, near the sites of these mills and the Revolutionary War battle of Fort Freeland, the second Warrior Run Church was built in 1789. The church was located in front of the present Warrior Run Church, built in 1835. The Warrior Run Church is the oldest denominational church in the

West Branch Valley. It is located at the eastern boundary of Delaware Township.

The town of Dewart grew during the mid 1800s after the opening of the Philadelphia and Erie Railroad (later the Pennsylvania Railroad). A warehouse was built along the railroad for the handling of grain. This warehouse was later enlarged and became the freight and passenger station. The first home of the post colonial era was built on Main Street in 1857, and the first store, operated by Abraham Benner, was built in 1858. The first hotel was built in 1859 by John H. Foresman, and later operated by the Mentz family. Soon, other tradesmen built and operated in Dewart, including a shoemaker, blacksmith, saddler, and wagon maker. (2)

Though the opening of the Philadelphia and Reading Railroad across the river at Allenwood slowed the shipping traffic at Dewart, the community continued to florish in the second half of the nineteenth century. C.T. Michener started a store on the north side of Main Street in 1875. This store was bought by George B. Sterner in 1901 and was operated by the Sterner family through most of the twentieth century. William Young opened a hardware store in 1893, which was operated by the Youngs for over a century. The Dewart Creamery was started in 1900 as a branch of the Sheffer Creamery at Muncy. It changed hands in 1946, becoming part of Penn Dairies, and was closed in 1966. (3)

On May 21, 1919 a tornado struck the Russell farm on the River Road at Dewart and also damaged several other buildings including the Dewart High School, formerly the Dewart Academy. Though the high school was destroyed, only two of the 17 pupils inside at the time were injured. The damage from the tornado attracted postcard photographers Nelson Caulkins and Lester Deininger. On the postcards the funnel cloud was called a cyclone, which was the lay term for tornado at that time. A new school was built in 1920. Damage to the Russell farm was repaired and the house and barn still stand today.

During the time that Nelson Caulkins had his studio in Watsontown, a rail disaster took place at Dewart. On November 23, 1918 two freight trains hit head-on in the night, making a massive display of destruction. Caulkins arrived early in the morning and took a series of six photographs while the smoke and steam were still in the air. The Caulkins Dewart train wreck photographs are among the best journalistic real photo postcards ever taken.

Between Turbotville and Montgomery, Route 54 crosses a stream, a branch of Delaware Run. On the west side of the stream, there is an inter-

This shaded street view of Dewart was taken by Nelson Caulkins, circa 1918.

157

section where Musser Lane meets Route 54 near the bridge. This area is called Delaware Run. At the intersection a brick one-room country school, the Delaware Run School, still stands. Just south of the intersection on Musser Lane is the St. John's Lutheran Church at Delaware Run. When the present church was built in 1867 it was called the St. John's Delaware Run Union Church. In the early 1900s, when it was photographed for post-cards, it was called the St. John's Church or River Church.

Delaware Township in the early 1900s provided the postcard photographers with many rural views to sell as postcards. Today, many of the buildings and scenes in the old postcards still remain.

*A **Swope real photo postcard** of Dewart, postmarked 1910.*

George B. Sterner's house *in Dewart. George B. Sterner was the grandfather of George N. Sterner who was postmaster and owner of Sterner's Store in the 1960s. Real photo postcard, circa 1910.*

East Main Street, Dewart. *Swope real photo postcard, circa 1908.*

Street view in Dewart. *Real photo postcard, circa 1910.*

C.M. Doebler's home in Dewart.   *Swope photo postcard, circa 1908.*

A house *in Dewart. Real photo postcard, circa 1910.*

Then: The Harley Mansion at Dewart. *This Swope Brothers photo postcard was taken by James Bannen Swope, circa 1908.*

Now: The Harley Mansion at Dewart *as photographed by the author in 2003. Harley was a medical doctor in the early 1900s.*

The Mentz Hotel, Dewart, Pa. *Swope real photo postcard, circa 1908. The brick structure was built as a hotel in 1859 by John H. Foresman. The Mentz family later bought it and operated a hotel there for many years. In the 1960s the building was the home and real estate office of Robert E. Hile. It still stands as a private home today.*

The Mentz Hotel *as viewed from the railroad tracks looking west. The building at the left margin is Brenner's General Store, later Hile's Grocery. Real photo postcard, early 1900s.*

A street scene in Dewart. *Caulkins real photo postcard, circa 1918.*

A team of horses *being led down the street in Dewart. Real photo postcard, circa 1915.*

The Dewart Creamery *was started in 1900 by David Gundrum, Harry J. Sheffer, and Charles F. Sheffer as a branch of the Sheffer Creamery of Muncy. Eventually Charles Sheffer purchased the entire Dewart operation. In 1946 the Dewart Creamery was bought by Penn Dairies and remained in business until 1966.*

The Dewart Creamery wagon. *Real photo postcard, circa 1910.*

A 1917 view of the Dewart Creamery C-cab REO truck. (See Thomas, Lewey and Mary Ellen, Moving On.)

Aftermath of the Dewart Creamery fire of 1925. The West Branch Fire Company of Watsontown had loaned the Silsby Steam Fire Engine to a fire company in Dewart. The Silsby fire engine was lost in this fire. Real photo postcard.

The Pennsylvania Railroad Station at Dewart. *Real photo postcard, circa 1910.*

The railroad station at Dewart, circa 1918. The station was on the Pennsylvania Railroad. Real photo postcard.

The Russell house *with the Dewart covered bridge across Delaware Run on the left, circa 1915. This is a rare, early photo postcard of the covered bridge at Dewart.*

A close-up view *of the covered bridge at Dewart, from the postcard above.*

An aerial view of Dewart. Real photo postcard.

Dewart EV. Church.

The Dewart Evangelical Church. *Swope real photo postcard, circa 1908. In 1946 the Evangelical Church merged with the United Brethren Church to form the Evangelical United Brethren Church (EVUB). In 1968 the EVUB merged with the Methodist Church to form the United Methodist. When the first merger occurred, the former Union Church on River Street in Dewart was in use as a United Brethren Church. The United Brethren Church was maintained and the former Evangelical Church on Main Street, shown above, was sold to the community to be used as a community center. The building is still in use, though it has been altered with an addition.*

Then: The Union Chapel *at Dewart, circa 1908. This is a Swope real photo postcard. At one time a United Brethren Church, today this church is the St. John's United Methodist Church.*

Now: The Union Church, *now the St. John's United Methodist Church as photographed by the author in 2003. This photograph shows the church before an addition was built in 2005.*

HIGH SCHOOL B'LD'G, DEWART, PA.

The high school building at Dewart, Pa. before May, 1919. This was the original Dewart High School, built in 1859 as a private academy near the Russell farm just north of the town. It was destroyed by a tornado (labeled on early postcards " cyclone") on May 21, 1919. The "new" Dewart school was built in 1920 east of town. Real photo postcard.

DEWART HIGH SCHOOL
DESTROYED BY CYCLONE MAY 21ST 1919
DEININGER   #1

The Dewart High School after it was destroyed by a tornado in May of 1919. At the time the tornado hit, I.H. Mauser, county superintendent of schools, Russell Kessler, principal, and 17 students were huddled on the first floor corridor. No one was killed but two students were slightly injured. (4) This is photo #1 of an outstanding five postcard series done by Watsontown photographer Lester Deininger.

170

Another view *of the tornado damage at the Dewart School. No. 2 of the Deininger five postcard series.*

View of the Dewart School *tornado damage. Real photo postcard*

The Edward Russell barn before the tornado struck on May 21, 1919. Real photo postcard.

A Caulkins real photo postcard showing the effects of the "cyclone" at Dewart in 1919.

EFFECT OF CYCLONE AT DEWART, PA. MAY 21st, '19,

A view taken from the railroad tracks of the Edward Russell farm after the tornado hit in May of 1919. A Caulkins real photo postcard.

Another postcard view *of tornado damage at the Russell farm.*

EFFECT OF CYCLONE AT DEWART, PA. MAY 21st, '19,
Caulkins Photo,

A Caulkins real photo postcard of the Russell farm after the tornado hit.

FARM BUILDINGS OF EDW. RUSSELL DEWART, PA.
DESTROYED BY CYCLONE MAY 21st 1910
DEININGER #3
PHOTO

Deininger photo postcard #3, showing tornado damage at the Russell farm at Dewart.

Barn of Edward Russell *of Dewart, destroyed by a tornado May 21, 1919. Deininger photo postcard #4.*

Fifth and last *of the Lester Deininger real photo postcard series depicting tornado damage at the Russell farm at Dewart.*

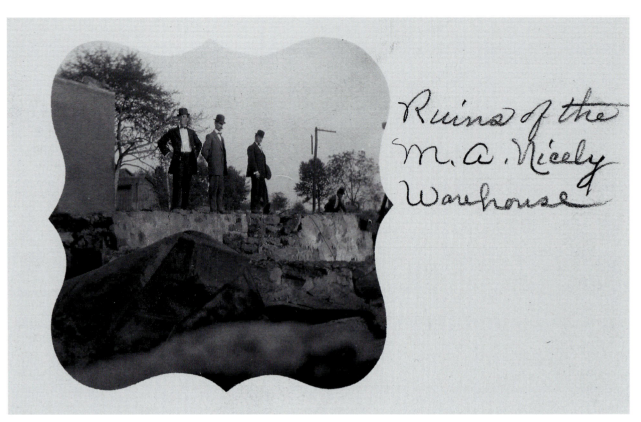

Ruins of the M.A. Nicely warehouse at Dewart. Real photo postcard.

Ruins of the Hotel Dewart. Real photo postcard.

THE DEWART TRAIN WRECK

On November 23, 1918, two freight trains collided head-on about a mile north of Dewart on the Pennsylvania Railroad. The wreck killed six employees and injured three. The wreck occurred at 4:15 a.m. and was photographed later that morning by Watsontown postcard photographer Nelson Caulkins.

About 4.00 a.m. Freight Extra 1478 with 79 loaded cars and one empty car passed a block tower a few miles west of Dewart heading eastbound on the westbound track of a double track. Extra 1478 was going against the normal flow of traffic on that track. The train was operating under train orders, which supercedes timetable instruction and block signal indication. In other words, handwritten train orders have priority over other forms of train instruction and signals, but the orders must be delivered in writing by a block operator. The operator places the order in a wooden train order hoop and hands it up to a trainman who leans from the train and hooks the hoop with his hand, quickly pulls the order from the hoop and then discards the empty hoop so the block operator can pick it up again and return to the tower. All of this happens in seconds while the train is still in motion. When a train order is directed by a dispatcher, the block operator forewarns the train crew to pick up an order by placing a train order light at his tower. The wreck occurred because a block operator neglected to deliver a train order to an oncoming train and allowed it to enter his block after Extra 1478 was already given the block.

The oncoming train, Extra 3510 consisting of an engine, tender and caboose passed Q Tower, about .7 miles east of Dewart, at 4:10 a.m. heading west on the same track as Extra 1478 heading east. No train order light was lit, no train order

was delivered, and no attempt was made by Operator Schrey at Q Tower to stop Extra 3510 from entering the same block as Extra 1478. At 4:15 a.m. Operator Schrey notified the dispatcher that he had forgotten about Extra 1478 and did not deliver the train order which would have halted Extra 3510 at Q Tower. He said that he had his order light up but that it went out and so allowed Extra 3510 to enter the block on a clear signal. Dispatcher Penny then called Operator Gresh at DE Tower west of Q tower and asked him if he could see Extra 1478. Gresh replied "only its (rear) markers." Penny, then fully aware that both trains were on a collision course, informed the trainmaster, and arranged to send out the wrecker.

At 4:15 a.m., the time the above conversations were taking place, the two trains collided just west of Dewart at a combined speed of 50 to 60 miles per hour. The two steam locomotive engines were instantly demolished. The first six cars of Extra 1478 were tank cars filled with fuel oil. The first car buckled with the tender and both ended upright. The two following cars broke open and fuel oil spilled everywhere and then caught fire. The caboose of Extra 3510 overturned and the pot belly caboose stove ignited the wooden cab and burned the entire structure. The engineman, fireman, and brakeman of Extra 1478 and the engineman, fireman, and conductor of Extra 3510 were killed.

An investigation later showed that Operator Schrey was negligent in his responsibilities, possibly encumbered from lack of sleep. Even though he was off duty for 16 hours before his shift, he testified that he had only about 4 hours sleep before coming to work. He had been suspended briefly the previous spring for sleeping on duty. (5)

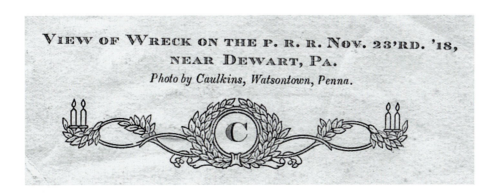

Nelson Caulkins' logo *from the back of one of his Dewart train wreck cabinet photographs.*

This set of six real photo postcards was made by Nelson Caulkins after a head-on collision between two freight trains on November 23, 1918. Caulkins printed these images as both postcards and cabinet photos.

Tender and tank car of Extra 1478 buckled, ending upright. The train cars protruding above the normal landscape provided Caulkins with an eerie subject.

Smoke rolled *from the burning debris. This view shows smoke from the burning fuel oil of the tank cars.*

Another Caulkins view *showing the smoke billowing from the wreckage.*

Caulkins view *of the train wreck. The front of Extra 1478 is at the right margin.*

Caulkins view #4 *showing the buckled cars.*

Delaware Run *near Dewart. Real photo postcard, postmarked 1914.*

Delaware Run *near Dewart. Real photo postcard, postmarked 1914.*

Then: ***A scene from the River Road*** *north of Dewart, postmarked 1907. Taken from the Susquehanna River bank in the northwest corner of Delaware Township, the postcard view shows the Pennsylvania Railroad bridge in the foreground and the cliffs at Montgomery in the background.*

Now: ***The same view*** *as above, taken by the author in 2006.*

Then: ***The Delaware Run School*** *located at the intersection of Route 54 and Musser Lane about 5 miles northwest of Turbotville. Real photo postcard, circa 1910.*

Now: ***The Delaware Run School*** *in 2003. Little has changed. Even the barn in the background remains. Photo by the author.*

Students at the Delaware Run School. *Real photo postcard, 1914.*

Six men at the crossroads *at the Delaware Run School. From left to right: Carl Stahlnecker, Wilbert Stahlnecker, Bill Nachauer, Warren Stahlnecker, Tom Ward, "Guinea" Nachauer. Real photo postcard.*

Then: The River Church *on Delaware Run about three miles north of Watsontown. (The church is located on Musser Lane 8/10 of a mile south of the intersection of Route 54, just south of the Delaware Run School.) During the 1800s this church was named the St. John's Union Church. This Swope Brothers real photo postcard, postmarked 1907, was taken by James Bannen Swope.*

Now: The River Church, *now called the St. John Evangelical Lutheran Church. This photograph was taken by the author in 2000.*

1816   Centennial Celebration   **1916**

St. John's (River) Church,

Delaware Township, Northumberland County,

Penna., June 17th and 18th, '16

Dear Friend:—You are cordially invited to attend the Centennial of St. John's Church, in the month of June. During the evenings of that week many former pastors will speak. Saturday, the seventeenth, will be an Old Home Day Picnic and Reminiscent Meeting. Sunday morning will be our Centennial Communion—the front seats being reserved for the oldest members and former members of St. John's. Sunday evening—An Historic Service.

Come Back to the Celebration

The Centennial Committee

Postcard announcing a church centennial celebration by the St. John's River Church in June of 1916.

The Bannen-Swope house along the McEwensville – Muncy road, just inside the eastern boundary of Delaware Township near Turbotville. Owned by postcard photographer James Bannen Swope during the first half of the twentieth century, the limestone house has been in the family continuously since the 1800s, having been purchased by the photographer's grandfather, James Bannen, about 1870. Completed in 1804 as a tavern, Henry Clay spoke from the front steps.

186

Then: **The Warrior Run Church,** *circa 1910, located in Delaware Township between Watsontown and Turbotville. Though the Warrior Run Church began at a temporary location in 1775, south of Watsontown, this structure, shown in the Ralph Fuller real photo postcard, was built in 1835.*

Now: The Warrior Run Church *today shows virtually no change from the early twentieth century Ralph Fuller view above. Photo taken by the author, 2003.*

The Warrior Run Church *in the early 1900s.*

Swope real photo postcard *of a Warrior Run Church picnic taken August 15, 1907.*

The Warrior Run Church in the mid 1950s. From a
color photograph taken by Ralph Fuller.

1775   **Grand Celebration**   1925
Watsontown==Warrior Run Church
July 18th and 19th, 1925

POST CARD

Place
2 Cent
Stamp
Here

Commemorating the 150th Anniversary of First
Regilious Service held on the West Branch of the
Susquehanna, July 16th, 1775.

Saturday 18th—Pilgrimage to Warrior Run
Church.

Program: 2 o'clock P. M. Historical address,
Hon. Frederick A. Godcharles. Music, Trate's Military Band, Chorus and Community Singing; Meeting of Old Friends. 8 o'clock P. M.—Front of City
Hall, Watsontown, Grand Band Concert.

Sunday, 19th, Watsontown, 5 o'clock P. M.—
Grand Parade, Churches and Sunday schools to
Memorial Park. Program: Address by Honorable
Emerson Collins. Music by Trate's Band, Chorus
and Community Singing.

You are Invited; a Royal Welcome awaits you.
Under auspices Municipal League.

FOR ADDRESS

A 1925 postcard commemorates the 150th anniversary of the Warrior Run Church, July 18 & 19,
1925.

POSTSCRIPT

From the onset this book was intended to be the ultimate finale as a postcard history of Watsontown, McEwensville and Delaware Township. That attitude soon dissolved as it did not take me long to realize how vast the postcard world really is. There would be some images, which for whatever reason, would not make it into this book. Also, if I continually looked for the next previously unknown postcard to emerge, the book would never get finished, as I would always be wondering if the next potential addition might be just around the corner. So, I had to make a cut off. This is it. This is the history. But history is never stagnant nor waits long for anyone. New history will emerge as hidden facts become known. In this case, someday there will probably have to be a supplement, or sequel, to this book, for its very existence will undoubtedly bring to attention more unpublished material. So, what I have presented here is a photo history of the area. Its completeness will be determined sometime in the future. For now, it is here for the enjoyment of us in the present.

Robert Swope, Jr.

Cabinet photo of the Charles Sheffer home on north Main Street, Watsontown. This photograph was taken by Arthur Ishiguro, a Milton photographer. It was found by the author in the Lewisburg Roller Mills Antique Marketplace the week before this book went into production.

NOTES

Chapter 1

1. Newspaper clipping, circa mid 1950s, on Nelson Caulkins, Caulkins Family Archives, maintained by Anne Lipe.

2. Interview with Anne Lipe, granddaughter of Nelson Caulkins, April, 2001.

3. Janyce B. Caulkins, *To Make a Long Story Short, Our Family History*, pp.48-50. Caulkins Family Tree, printed June, 2001.

4. Interview with Anne Lipe, April, 2001.

5. Caulkins, *To Make…*, p.49.

6. Interview with Marvin Wolfe of Slate Run, Pa., summer, 2001.

7. Caulkins, *To Make…*, p.50.

8. Interview with Anne Lipe, April, 2001. Interviews with Jerry and Ronnie Yothers, 2005-2006.

9. Interviews with Neoska Fuller Campbell, 2002-2004. Ralph Fuller Archives, photographs and notes.

10. Fuller Archives. Interview with Neoska Campbell.

11. Interviews with Neoska Campbell. Interviews with Janet Hause of Turbotville.

12. Fuller Archives, letter written by Ralph Fuller, September 2, 1972.

13. Interviews with Lester Swope, 2002-2005. Interviews with Paul Swope of Chicago Heights, Illinois, 2002-2004.

14. Fuller Archives, school related papers. Lewis Township Tax Record Books, 1901-1908.

15. Interviews with Paul Swope, 2002-2004. Notes from Paul Swope, April, 2003.

16. Notes from Paul Swope, April, 2003.

17. Interviews with Harold McCollin, 2004. Interviews with Harry Carson, 2002-2004. Watsontown Cemetery records.

18. *Genealogical and Biographical Annals of Northumberland County, Pennsylvania*, pp.322-323.

19. *Genealogical…*, pp.322, 323. Interviews with Helen Schuyler, 2005-2006.

20. Robert Scott Franks, *Difficult Crossing*, pp.iv,v.

21. Franks, *Difficult…*, pp.162,163.

22. Marlin Thomas, *Lewey and Mary Ellen, Moving On*, p.49. Interview with Marlin Thomas, 2006.

23. Thomas, *Lewey…*, p.53.

24. Thomas, *Lewey…*, pp.61-64.

25. Several of the images here are published in Thomas's book *Lewey and Mary Ellen*. Scans of the originals were sent to the author by Mr. Thomas.

26. Harold Nesbit photograph albums from the Benion auction, Milton, summer, 2005.

27. Interview with Josephine Nesbit, 2006. Additional photos by Nesbit of the White Deer – Watsontown bridge opening are published in Robert Franks' and Karen Houser's *A Landmark Reborn*, a book about the renovation of the bridge and a sequel to Franks' book *Difficult Crossing*.

Chapter 2

1. *Watsontown, 1867 – 1967*, centennial history, Early History section.

2. *Watsontown…*, Early History.

3. *Watsontown…*, Industrial History of Watsontown.

4. *Watsontown…*, Industrial History of Watsontown.

5. *Watsontown…*, Industrial History of Watsontown.

6. *Watsontown…*, Industrial History of Watsontown.

7. *Watsontown…*, Our Schools.

8. *Watsontown…*, Our Churches.

9. *Watsontown...*, Local Government. *Bicentennial Reprint of Old Home Week*, Watsontown Historically section.
10. Frederic L. Paxson, ed., *War Cyclopedia, A Handbook for Ready Reference on the Great War*, pp.231-233.
11. Camp Fire USA Law website.
12. Alice Marie Beard, Bethesda, Md., Historical Origins of Camp Fire website.

Chapter 3

1. Agnes I. Beard, *History of McEwensville*, p.1.
2. Beard, *History...*, p.1.
3. Beard, *History...*, Beginnings section written by Mrs. Robert Callenberger, pp.5-10.
4. *Genealogical and Biographical Annals of Northumberland County, Pennsylvania*, p.921.
5. Interview with Neoska Fuller Campbell, 2003.
6. Beard, *History...*, pp.2,3.
7. Notes on the Susquehanna, Bloomsburg, and Berwick Railroad, accumulated 1999-2003.
8. J. Stephen Gold, *The Gold Family in America*, pp.139-163.

Chapter 4

1. *Watsontown, 1867 – 1967*, centennial history, Delaware Township section.
2. *Watsontown...*, Delaware Township.
3. *Watsontown...*, Delaware Township.
4. *Watsontown...*, Delaware Township.
5. Pennsylvania Railroad Volume I, ICC Accident Reports, 1911 – 1930, section entitled "In RE Investigation of an Accident Which Occurred on the Pennsylvania Railroad near Dewart, Pa. on November 23, 1918."

BIBLIOGRAPHY

Beard, Agnes I., *History of McEwensville*, McEwensville, Pa., 1945.

Beitler, Lewis E., editor, *Fiftieth Anniversary of the Battle of Gettysburg, Report of the Pennsylvania Commission*, Harrisburg, Pa., 1915.

Blake, Jody, Lasansky, Jeannette, *Rural Delivery, Real Photo Postcards from Central Pennsylvania, 1905 – 1935*, Union County Historical Society, Lewisburg, Pa., 1996.

Caulkins, Janyce B., *To Make a Long Story Short, Our Family's History*, Hampton, Virginia, 1998.

Dersham, Arna, *The History of White Deer Township*, White Deer Bicentennial Commission, White Deer, Pa., 1976.

Franks, Robert Scott, *Difficult Crossing*, West Branch Heritage, Watsontown, Pa., 2004.

Franks, Robert Scott, Houser, Karen Y., *A Landmark Reborn*, West Branch Heritage, Watsontown, Pa., 2006.

Gold, Stephen J., *The German Golds in America*, ABC Printing, Bethlehem, Pa., 1971.

Kramm, Thomas S., *The History of the McEwensville Schools, 1800 – 1958*, Thompsontown, Pa., 2000.

Paxson, Frederic L., editor, *War Cyclopedia, A Handbook for Ready Reference on the Great War*, Government Printing Office, Washington, D.C., 1918.

Shank, William H., *The Amazing Pennsylvania Canals*, American Canal & Transportation Center, York, Pa., 1981.

Swartz, Roger G., Fields of Honor: *The Battle of Fort Freeland, July 28, 1779*, Warrior Run – Fort Freeland Heritage Society, Turbotville, Pa., 1996.

Taber, Thomas T., III, *Sunset Along Susquehanna Waters*, Muncy, Pa., 1972.

Thomas, Marlin, *Lewey and Mary Ellen, Moving On*, King George, Va., 2005.

Willoughby, Martin, *A History of Postcards*, Wellfleet Press, Secaucus, New Jersey, 1992.

_____ *Bicentennial Reprint of Old Home Week* (original booklet published in 1915), Watsontown National Bank, Watsontown, Pa., 1975.

_____ *Genealogical and Biographical Annals of Northumberland County, Pennsylvania*, J.S. Floyd & Co., Chicago, 1911.

_____ *The Lanthorn, '10 – Vol. XIII*, Susquehanna University, Selinsgrove, Pa., 1910.

_____ *Milton, Pennsylvania 1905*, picture book of Milton, 1905.

_____ *Turbotville Centennial, 1859 – 1959*, Turbotville, Pa., 1959.

_____ *Watsontown, 1867 – 1967*, Watsontown Centennial Committee, Watsontown, Pa., 1967.

_____ *Watsontown's 2nd Historic Walking Tour, Sat. May 31, 1980*, Watsontown Guild, Watsontown, Pa., 1980.

Wolfe, Rick, papers on the history of Watsontown, published yearly, 1992 – 2001.

Pennsylvania Railroad, Vol. I, ICC Accident Reports, 1911 – 1930, CD, Media Surplus, Kearney, Mo., 2003.

Beard, Alice Marie, Historical Origins of Camp Fire. Website, http://members.aol.com/alicebeard/campfire/history.html, Bethesda, Md.

Camp Fire USA Law. Website, http://www.campfireusaihc.org/campfireusalaw.html

POSTCARD AND PHOTOGRAPH INDEX